The Travels of Captain Cook

THE TRAVELS OF

WERNER FORMAN
RONALD SYME

CAPTAIN
COOK

McGraw-Hill Book Company
New York · Toronto

This book was produced
by COPRO INTERNATIONAL Verlagsges. m.b.H., Vienna

Graphic design: Franz X. Eder, Vienna

CONTENTS

Published by order of the Lords Commissioners of the Admiralty.
London, W. and A. Strahan, 1784.

Select Bibliography

Captain Cook's Journal during his first voyage round the world made in H. M. bark "Endeavour" 1768–71.
London, Elliot Stock, 1893

John Hawkesworth: *An Account of the voyages undertaken by the order of his present Majesty for making Discoveries in the Southern Hemisphere, and successively performed by Byron, Wallis, Carteret and Cook.*
London, Strahan, 1773.
Three volumes.

Johann Georg Adam Forster: *A voyage round the World, in His Britannic Majesty's Sloop "Resolution," commanded by Captain James Cook, during the years 1772–75.*
London, W. Strahan, 1777.
Two volumes.

Arthur Kitson: *Captain James Cook.* London, 1907

R. T. Gould: *Captain Cook,* London, 1935

Hugh Carrington: *Life of Captain Cook.* London, Sidgwick & Jackson, 1939

J. A. Williamson: *Cook and the Opening of the Pacific.* London, 1946

Alan Villiers: *Captain Cook, the seaman's seaman.* A study of the great discoverer. Illustr. by Adrian Small. London, Hodder & Stoughton, 1967

Raleigh Ashlin Skelton and Ronald Vere Tooley: *The marine Surveys of James Cook in North America 1758–1768.* Particularly the survey of Newfoundland. A bibliography of printed charts and sailing directions. London, The Map Collectors' Circle, 1967

Sources of the quotations:

The Journals of Captain James Cook on his voyages of discovery.
Edited from the original manuscript bei John Cawte Beaglehole.
Cambridge, University Press.
Vol. I, 1955: The first voyage
Vol. II, 1961: The second voyage
Vol. III, 1967: The third voyage

A Voyage to the Pacific Ocean.
Undertaken, by the command of his Majesty, for making discoveries in the Northern Hemisphere. To determine the position and extent of the West Side of North America; its distance from Asia; and the practicability of a Northern Passage to Europe.
Performed under the direction of Captains Cook, Clerke and Gore, In his Majesty's ships the Resolution and Discovery.
In the Years 1776, 1777, 1778, 1779 and 1780.
In three volumes.
Vol. I. and II. written by Captain James Cook, F.R.S.
Vol. III. by Captain James King, LL.D. and F.R.S.
Illustrated with maps and charts, from the original drawings made by Lieut. Henry Roberts, under the direction of Captain Cook; and with a great variety of portraits of persons, views of places, and historical representations of remarkable incidents, drawn by Mr. Webber during the voyage, and engraved by the most eminent artists.

Ye Son of a Day Labourer

October 27, 1728. James, Ye Son of a Day Labourer, James Cook, and of his wife, Grace.

he entry was made in the leather-bound parish register and the ink in the scrawled line of writing duly sanded. The parents trudged homeward, carrying their newly baptized son wrapped in a warm shawl to protect him against the chill wind. The handful of witnesses and the black-coated vicar departed along the lonely highroad leading to the nearby village of Marton-cum-Cleveland. The dumpy, stone-walled little church of St. Cuthbert in the rolling, grassy Yorkshire plain became silent and deserted.

The baptism had been a humble, insignificant incident in the daily lives of the villagers. James Cook was a hired laborer on the moderately prosperous farm of a country gentleman named Scottowe, but as he had no family in the district—it was said that he came from somewhere north of the Scottish border—no one knew much about him. His twenty-three-year-old wife, Grace, a decent, modest, hard-working woman, was equally obscure. She was English, her maiden name may have been Vace, and this latest child was her second son. The couple lived in a two-room, earthen-walled cottage on the Scottowe farm. James, her husband, was a big-built, serious-minded fellow, wise in the ways of livestock and crops, and much trusted by his employer. He may have been able to write a little, but lack of education was of no great consequence in those grudging times.

The fields became yellow with approaching winter. The gnarled hawthorns along the winding lanes were covered with red berries, and the names of other newly baptized infants followed those of

James Cook in the parish register. The tranquil life of the peaceful countryside continued unchanged. The world was unaware that one of the greatest maritime explorers of all time had just been born.

During the first part of the eighteenth century, while James was learning to walk and then to carry out his share of simple household tasks, the scientific world of Europe was not unduly interested in Pacific exploration. The vast ocean remained merely a cipher that, as all sensible men realized, would one day have to be solved.

The voyages of exploration during the fifteenth and sixteenth centuries brought the Pacific to the attention of geographers. It was discovered and crossed for the first time by Ferdinand Magellan, who lost his life in the process.

Magellan's voyage inaugurated a race for the discovery of the new continent that was said to exist somewhere in the southern hemisphere. First the Spanish and Portuguese, then the Dutch, French, and English. From these navigators and explorers three names emerge with great distinction: Magellan who showed the way; Tasman who established the existence of New Zealand, Australia, and Tasmania; and James Cook who was soon to chart the discoveries of earlier explorers in addition to making a great many discoveries of his own.

The first Pacific navigators followed much the same course across that ocean. They sailed from Europe, rounded Cape Horn, and then sailed westward between the equator and the Tropic of Capricorn, sighting on the way some of the Tuamotu Islands, New Guinea, and the Philippines. From the time of Magellan's voyage until the early eighteenth century, this route remained almost unaltered owing to the ships' having to take advantage of the most favorable winds with as little delay as possible. In this manner, the Tuamotus, Marquesas, Tongas, New Hebrides, and Solomons were all discovered. So were numerous other unknown atolls and islands, including Easter Island and Pitcairn.

Interest about the Pacific was stimulated in England in 1694 by the publication of Tasman's journal, and still further aroused three years later by the publication of Dampier's *New Voyage Round the World*. Dampier, to whose memory the world has paid little of the honor due, made four tremendous voyages and completed three circumnavigations of the globe. But it was not until 1764 that Captain Byron of the British Navy performed a purely exploratory voyage round the world, which he completed in 1766. Four months later a more ambitious expedition, consisting of Captain Samuel Wallis in the *Dolphin* and Captain Carteret in the *Swallow*, carried out a further circumnavigation, during which Wallis discovered Tahiti in the Society Islands.

The foundation of the South Sea Company in 1711 had already provided an indication that the British government was contemplating the commercial possibilities of the Pacific, but within thirty years this company had become nothing but a name. Captain Byron's voyage around the world, followed by that of Samuel Wallis, had rather shaken British faith in the theory of the alleged southern continent. That faith was not to manifest itself again until the conclusion of peace after the Seven Years' War in 1763. Britain then decided that something would really have to be done to chart the Pacific in a proper manner.

Meanwhile life began treating the Cook family with reasonable generosity. James Cook, senior, was made bailiff of a larger farm belonging to Mr. Scottowe at Great Ayton, four miles from Marton-cum-Cleveland. There he lived with his wife and the seven children* who had arrived after his son James, in a neat and sturdy cottage built with

---

* Of all nine children, in addition to James only the first-born son, John, and a twenty-year younger sister, Margaret, survived childhood.

walls of yellow-grey stone quarried from the Cleveland Hills. His wages rose with the passing years so that the family always had enough to eat during even the cold, fruitless winter months.

The younger James also began doing well for himself. The frugal ways he learned as a small boy were beginning to stand him in good stead. Mr. Scottowe, with a generosity unfortunately rare in those days, paid for the boy's education at the Ayton village school. James learned to read and write fluently—though not to spell accurately—and acquired considerable ability in simple arithmetic. At the age of seventeen, after some obstinate arguments with his father, he became a grocer's assistant in the nearby coastal village of Staithes.

A year and a half in a dingy little shop in a grey, windswept village was enough for James. At the age of eighteen, a tall, heavy-shouldered, taciturn and steady young man, he obtained employment with a Quaker shipping firm, Walkers of Whitby, and went to sea as an apprentice on the five-hundred-ton collier, *Freelove*.

A flair for mathematics and the ability to learn competent pilotage in the detestable North Sea rewarded young James Cook handsomely. So did his obvious honesty, reliability, and enduring efforts to improve his education.

He was promoted to mate at twenty-three. The approving, kindly Walkers were giving him every possible chance. He carried out his orders precisely as he was told and left planning and talking to others. His cautious navigation in fog, gales, and along treacherous rock-girt coasts, which yearly claimed a heavy toll of men and ships, was faultless. His personal habits were sober, modest, and altogether admirable. The Walkers were soon planning to give him command of their new vessel that was already on the stocks. As good, prosperous Quakers, interested in little except commerce, they entirely overlooked the possible significance of the outbreak of the Seven Years' War in 1756.

James did not. A naval war was the opportunity he had awaited. That war was now beginning and it might last for years. The British Navy was already

9

desperately in need of trained seamen. In those days Naval promotion depended not so much on one's knowledge of seamanship as on family name and useful connections. Any misguided young gentleman who decided to become a Naval officer usually did so merely because he lacked sufficient means to live in elegant manner ashore. "Ye son of a day labourer," totally lacking influential friends and private income, might have a very hard time indeed in securing any worthwhile promotion even in wartime.

There was certainly no need for Cook to have joined the Navy. As senior officer of a merchant ship he was safe from the pressgangs who even then were busy raiding filthy dives and the stews of revolting slums in search of those criminal, gin-sodden wretches who, as seamen afloat, maintained—surprisingly—the supremacy of the British Navy.

The war did not begin officially until 1756, but in the summer of 1755 British and French squadrons were already exchanging broadsides. Privateers of both nations were making the high seas dangerous for merchant shipping.

On 17 June 1755 James Cook, not yet twenty-seven, and until recently mate of the fine big *Freelove* —she was considerably larger than the *Endeavour* of later years—joined the Navy as an obscure able-bodied seaman.

He had sacrificed his rank and excellent prospects. His pay as a Naval seaman, provided the Navy duly remembered to pay him at all, was an insignificant fraction of his wages on the collier. He had taken the biggest gamble of his life after shrewdly assessing his personal handicaps and qualifications.

In an efficiently run Navy, the latter would have ensured his rapid promotion to commissioned rank. Not only was he highly competent in practical navigation; he understood the complex theory on which it was based. In the damp discomfort of his tiny cabin aboard the collier, he had engaged in unremitting study every night until his eyes ached and his head became giddy from the steady perusal of the charts and logarithms and trigonometric calculations necessary to mark with accuracy the tiny dot that represented a ship's position on an empty ocean.

But the Navy was not efficiently run. Cook's flair for navigation, the admirable punctuation and phrasing of his log, even his hard-won ability to express himself fluently and correctly in King's English, might be discounted in favor of some self-assured and slightly bored young aristocrat who could rely on powerful family connections to offset his ignorance of logarithms and unhandiness with a sextant.

The one circumstance in Cook's favor was the fact that the Navy was now entering upon a strenuous period of war. Not even a stuffy and hidebound Admiralty, where tradition was hallowed above all things, cared to entrust a valuable ship to incompetent officers and crew. Good men were suddenly at a premium.

"I had a mind," said Cook tersely, "to try my fortune that way."

His gamble paid off handsomely.

The dark, damp hellhole where the crew swung their hammocks aboard the *Eagle*, sixty guns and four hundred men, was his introduction to the Navy. Even the height of this orlop deck, a mere five feet six inches, was an added burden to a six-footer like Cook. But he was out of it for good inside of a month.

Captain Sir Hugh Palliser, a competent and professional veteran, was delighted to find a real seaman amongst the crowd of loutish, seasick, and unhandy landlubbers who comprised the majority of his crew. A month after joining the ship, Cook was abruptly promoted to master's mate. Six months later he was again promoted, this time to boatswain— a position of considerable responsibility aboard a large ship.

In the summer of 1757, two years after joining the Navy, Cook was made master of the *Pembroke*, a 64-gun ship of the line.

The master held the rank of warrant officer. His duties included the pilotage and navigation of the ship, and a general supervision and control of the crew. It was a rank where any blundering in-

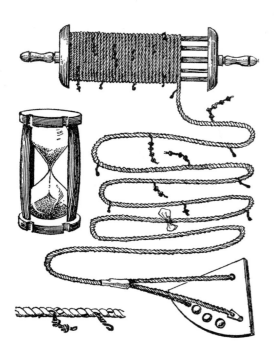

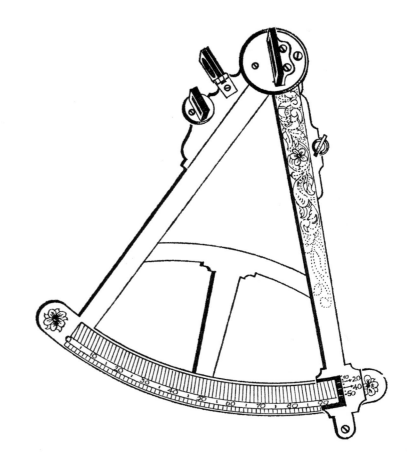

Among the most important equipment on sailing ships in Cook's time were the log chip, to gauge speed through the water; the sextant, to determine location; the compass, to maintain direction; and, of course, the guns.

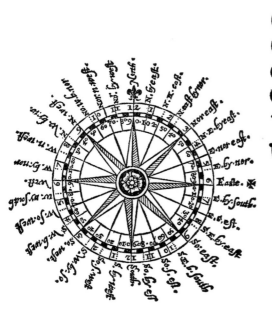

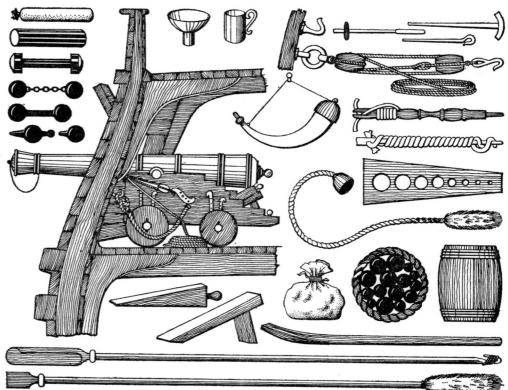

competent would quickly be revealed. The man who held it had to be a sound navigator and a natural disciplinarian.

At the beginning of 1759, the *Pembroke* was ordered to join the fleet which conveyed the army of Generals Wolfe and Amherst to North America. A grand attack on Quebec was being planned, and a Naval squadron under the command of Admiral Sir Charles Saunders was ordered to navigate its passage up the broad, winding and unpredictable St. Lawrence River.

As navigator and sailing master, Cook had a sudden increase in his already heavy burden of responsibility. The few French charts which the British Navy had contrived to obtain were by no means complete. Captured local French pilots were obviously not to be trusted. The boats of the British fleet had to perform all the surveying as if the great river were a new discovery; the channels had to be carefully buoyed so that the great lumbering ships could cautiously follow such markers as they advanced upstream.

Cook's part in the campaign was essential but certainly not spectacular. His chief piece of work, for which he attracted favorable official notice, consisted of sounding and buoying the broad stretch of river known as the Traverse, near Quebec, where the heaviest ships could safely swing at anchor. It was a dangerous spot. The channel shifted abruptly from the north to the south side of the river but confused this change of course in a maze of dangerous obstructions.

"9th June: Ye boats of ye fleet engaged in sounding ye channel of ye Traverse.

11th June: Ret'd satisfied with being acquainted with ye Channel."

Little mention was made in Cook's private diary of his dangerous cut-and-run skirmishing with intrepid French boat parties, of General Wolfe in person consulting him about the most suitable approach to a landing place, and no mention at all of the fact that official historians of the campaign were beginning to refer to him as the "master surveyor and master of the fleet"—an unrecognized title but highly significant of the respect in which he was held. He was worth a lot more to the Navy than the five shillings a day it agreed to pay him at highly irregular intervals and always in arrears.

The siege of Quebec ended on 13 September 1759. That day on the Plains of Abraham disciplined British infantry broke the gallant blue-uniformed ranks of the advancing French troops with an admirably timed volley and a series of irresistible bayonet charges. With this battle the conflict between the French and the English settlers, which had lasted for decades, was decided.

Once the fighting was over, Cook produced a survey of the lower St. Lawrence River which, by virtue of its accuracy, quickly superseded all the older charts. It won him a high reputation as the finest navigator in the Navy, and promotion to the rank of master to the Admiral's flagship, the *Northumberland*.

"From my experience of Mr. Cook's genius and capacity," wrote the *Northumberland*'s captain, Lord Colville, "I think him well qualified for the work he has performed and for greater undertakings of the same kind."

Those "greater undertakings" were not yet on Cook's horizon. The Admiralty had a regulation that no seaman could be granted a commission aboard a king's ship until he had served on such a vessel for at least six years.

Admiralty regulations were unbreakable. Mr. James Cook had not completed the necessary length of service. In any case it seemed that the present war might end within the next year or two. The demand for highly skilled seamen was already abating; in the blessed event of peace, England, in traditional manner, would leave them to become two for a penny.

South Latitude

I n November 1762, when the war was in its last stages, the *Northumberland* returned to England. Cook was paid off, along with the rest of the crew, receiving just under £ 300 from the Admiralty. The sum was worth perhaps ten or twelve times what it is today, and for the first time in his life, he found himself at leisure and with adequate funds in his pocket.

He was thirty-four years old. One month after his return, so it must have been a swift courtship, he married a twenty-one-year-old London girl, Elizabeth Batts, the daughter of a small shopkeeper.

She remained an insubstantial figure during Cook's life. Biographers have sought vainly for information regarding Elizabeth that would have made her a woman of flesh and blood in the pages of history, but none has succeeded. She remains as inconspicuous as the details of their wedding in the Parish Church of Little Barking on the untidy outskirts of eighteenth-century London. A few months later, they moved into a small house that Cook had bought in the Mile End Road.

That part of London is dismal and dilapidated today, but in 1763, a number of green fields, low-lying and wet though they were, must have been visible from the windows of the house. Cook had married well above the stratum in life to which he had been born; in the intricate social system of the day, a shopkeeper ranked very much higher than the son of a farm laborer. As a Naval warrant officer with a careful young wife installed in a house of their own, Cook was rising rapidly above his humble origin. His only concern was centered on his future in the Navy. Early in 1763 the Treaty of Paris ended the Seven Years' War, and his future career at sea remained for him a matter of doubt and some misgiving.

He was more fortunate than most of his contemporaries. All those chilly days he had spent sounding the icy waters of the St. Lawrence would prove to be a good investment.

A certain Captain Thomas Graves had been appointed Governor of Newfoundland. The coastline of that cold and isolated colony was imperfectly charted. Fishing boats from England, searching for cod with which to fill their capacious holds, were always coming to grief on unsuspected shoals and wave-covered reefs. Graves, who had taken part in the Quebec campaign, knew of Cook's brilliant work as a surveyor and asked for him now in order to have the shores of the colony properly mapped.

The cumbersome machinery of the Admiralty functioned with unusual celerity. Only four months after his marriage, Cook was appointed surveyor at the unusual salary of ten shillings a day. He was officially entitled "Mr. James Cook, Engineer," and also as "the King's Surveyor" supplied with an excellent set of surveying instruments and even an assistant. Perhaps even more to his pleasure, he was given the command of a tiny schooner called the *Grenville* with a complement of ten men. The only disappointment for him was that the frugal Admiralty, always worrying about seniority and expense, refused to give Mr. James Cook any added promotion.

Sir Hugh Palliser, Cook's old captain and influential patron, replaced Graves as Governor of Newfoundland in 1764. It was a harmonious working partnership. Palliser did everything in his power to assist Cook in his work, and allowed him to sail the little *Grenville* home to England at the end of every summer. After laying-up the ship in the Thames, Cook was able to spend the next four months at his home in the Mile End Road, where he busied himself with correlation of the charts and soundings he had recorded during the previous summer. It was dreary work, but at least he had the satisfaction of seeing some of his new charts published in the *Atlantic Pilot*. He also submitted a highly technical report on an eclipse of the sun to the *Transactions of the Royal Society*, in the pages of which he was introduced as "Mr. Cook, a good mathematician, very expert in his business."

Cook had come a long way in the ten years that had passed since he left the collier *Freelove*. He had already carved out a scientific niche for himself in the field of navigation and astronomy, and he had done so almost without a setback.

The one exception occurred during the summer of 1765 in Newfoundland. While standing on the deck of the *Grenville* one day in August, he had a large powder flask inexplicably to explode in his hand.

His loyal crew, very conscious of the fact that they had a humane and conscientious commander, crammed on all possible sail and rushed him to a small port on the coast where a competent French surgeon happened to be staying.

If the accident had occurred in a civilized country and resulted in Cook's being conveyed to one of the charnel houses technically known as hospitals, he would have been lucky if he had lost only his arm by amputation. The germ-laden scalpels and saws of the medical butchers would almost certainly have introduced the bacteria of pyaemia, or probably gangrene, into his bloodstream. In the cold, clean air and healthy surroundings of Newfoundland, he had an incomparably better chance of survival.

The surgeon made a handy job of sewing up the thumb that was almost severed from the rest of the hand, and the great wound healed perfectly. Only a heavy scar was left. It was to have its uses. Fifteen years later, it was this scar which enabled his crew to identify his body after the Polynesians of Hawaii had completely dismembered it.

France had lost her empire in North America. She was understandably anxious to found a new one in order to recoup the loss. Prominent French scientists, navigators, and politicians were still pondering the monumental work, *Histoire des Navigations aux Terres Australes* which Charles de Brosses had published in 1756, just as the Seven Years' War was beginning. The book outlined the history of all the known voyages to Australia, then known as New Holland, and the South Pacific. De Brosses submitted the theory that parts of a yet undiscovered southern continent, or *Terra Australis Incognita*, would be found to possess a favorable climate and

Cook's signature ending the journal of his second voyage.

vegetation suitable for European inhabitation. He even suggested, with an originality centuries ahead of his time, that possibly the natives of those countries might be able to teach the white races a useful thing or two. Unfortunately he went even further by suggesting that France would be able to deport her criminal and vicious elements to these countries, so that by contact with Nature, a mild climate, and a new green world free of civilized vice, they would be unconsciously purged of their evil instincts. The first part of the suggestion remained in the minds of his readers, the rest of it they ignored, at least for the time being.

At the end of the Seven Years' War, an English literary pirate named John Callender secured de Brosses' book and published an English version of it. Naturally he altered portions of the text so that Britain was named as the colonizing power instead of France. He did so, of course, without permission from de Brosses, to whom indeed he gave the most scanty and discourteous recognition.

The impact of de Brosses' great academic work was felt even by the British government. It was resolved that a search should be made for the southern continent. In 1766, Captain Wallis was sent out in the *Dolphin* and Captain Philip Carteret in the *Swallow*—a thirty-year-old, dilapidated little ship which a cautious navigator would have hesitated to sail round Britain—and ordered to try to locate the southern continent. They were to search the area northwest of Cape Horn, thus probably entering tropical latitudes in the Pacific.

Wallis, who appears to have deliberately lost contact with Carteret off the Cape, sailed towards the Tropic of Capricorn, whither warmer weather,

15

a prevailing easterly wind, and the existence of small islands providing fresh water and vegetables for his scurvy-ridden crew drew him like a magnet. The *Dolphin* was the second copper-sheathed ship owned by the Navy and she was a reasonably fast sailer.

In latitude 17° south, at a point midway between the west coast of South America and New Guinea, Wallis sighted Tahiti, the largest island discovered by any European since Tasman found New Zealand. It had a circumference of 125 miles.

With the lack of imagination invariably displayed by British explorers, Wallis named Tahiti King George the Third's Island. After introducing the unfortunate Polynesians of that island to the blessings of civilization, including death by gunfire and gonorrhea, Wallis sailed away via the Ladrones, Batavia, and the Indian Ocean to England.

Carteret, still plugging away in the slow, decayed and entirely unsuitable *Swallow*, kept a more southerly course than Wallis across the Pacific, discovering a few islands, such as Pitcairn, during the voyage. More important, however, was the fact that he sailed for sixty degrees of longitude across the theoretical continent of *Terra Australis* so beloved by geographers, thereby establishing fairly conclusively that it did not exist. Later he swung north to pass through the Solomon Islands and thence to Batavia, present day Djakarta. He finally reached England almost a year later than Captain Wallis.

Eight months after the latter discovered Tahiti, a professional French diplomat and soldier, de Bougainville by name, also reached Tahiti in the course of a voyage round the world. He named the beautiful island, which in those times was covered with beautiful forest to its highest peaks, New Cythera. Being an aristocrat and a man of letters, the unspoiled loveliness of Tahiti had a great effect on his sensitive feelings. He wrote of it as "another Eden, an Utopia, an Arcadia in which the Noble Savage behaved and looked like the Greek gods."

The race for the Pacific Ocean was now on. Both Britain and France were determined to seize all valuable territories before her rival country claimed them.

CAPTIONS OF PLATES 1, 2

1 *"Mr. Kendalls Watch now on board."*
The Royal Observatory at Greenwich, built in 1675, where astronomical work was actively pursued until 1948. It has been reopened as a museum, and here Cook's chronometer, constructed by Kendall, is still keeping perfect time.
2 *"Light breezes and fine weather."*
On the way to the far South.

H. M. S. Endeavour

he geographers of both countries continued to debate the existence or otherwise of *Terra Australis*, but at this stage Britain's territorial ambitions were stimulated still further by news from an unexpected quarter.

Some eighty years earlier, an English astronomer named Edward Halley had predicted that in 1769 the planet Venus would pass between the earth and the sun. If this transit were accurately observed, it would be possible to calculate the distance of one from the other. The entire scientific world was vastly interested in this matter. Nevil Maskelyne, the Astronomer Royal, declared that an observatory on the North Cape of Norway and another on the shores of Hudson Bay would provide adequate data from a northern latitude. Southern observations, Maskelyne added, could be obtained only on or extremely close to the Tropic of Capricorn and roughly halfway between Chile and the Dutch East Indies.

Armed with this data, the Royal Society applied to King George III for royal assistance in the matter. The king undertook to provide a subsidy of £ 4000 and also a Naval vessel. This was on 29 February 1768. On that same day, the Secretary of State informed the Admiralty that it was the king's intention to provide the proposed expedition to the South Pacific with a suitable vessel.

Almost before this message had been passed, Alexander Dalrymple, at the age of thirty a Fellow of the Royal Society, began to create trouble.

Dalrymple had served in Madras with the East India Company and risen to the command of one of their lumbering great merchantmen. Like many other unusually learned men, he had a peculiar kink. He believed in *Terra Australis* to the point of fanaticism, and would tolerate no expression of doubt on the matter. Dalrymple was convinced that Tasman's New Zealand was part of this southern continent, the coastline of which ran westward to Davis Land near the Chilean side of the South Pacific. Without any reasonable additional proof whatsoever, Dalrymple insisted that this coastline actually existed. He had so impressed the Royal Society as a competent geographer, sailor, and astronomer that they agreed rather weakly to his accompanying the Naval ship on its voyage to the South Pacific.

This was not good enough for Mr. Dalrymple. He insisted that he be placed in command of the vessel so that to him would accrue great honor as the discoverer of *Terra Australis*.

At this point a first-class row began between the Admiralty and Dalrymple himself. Only twice in its long history had the Admiralty entrusted command of one of its ships to a mere civilian. Once it had been Halley the astronomer, and once William Dampier the ex-buccaneer. Both voyages had ended in mutiny. The Navy had had enough. Never again would it allow anyone but a regular Naval officer to command one of its ships, and the Admiralty said so bluntly to Dalrymple. He was, they added, quite welcome to sail as the chief scientific observer of the transit.

Dalrymple haughtily refused this invitation and withdrew in cold hauteur from the entire project. His indignation was still further increased when he learned that an almost unknown Naval officer was to take command. Gentlemen in those days did not take kindly to being superseded by obscure commoners.

The Admiralty had already made up its own mind. The Secretary knew of Cook's work as a surveyor, and was also aware that this tall, burly Yorkshireman had sailed the tiny *Grenville* ten times across the Atlantic without misadventure of any kind. He asked Sir Hugh Palliser for an opinion, and that very senior officer agreed. After that the Navy no longer hesitated. Apart from everything else in Cook's favor, it was generally known that in some remarkable way he managed to keep his crews alive instead of allowing them to die of scurvy; not one of the *Grenville*'s crew had ever contracted a touch of the disease. It was really rather remarkable how he did

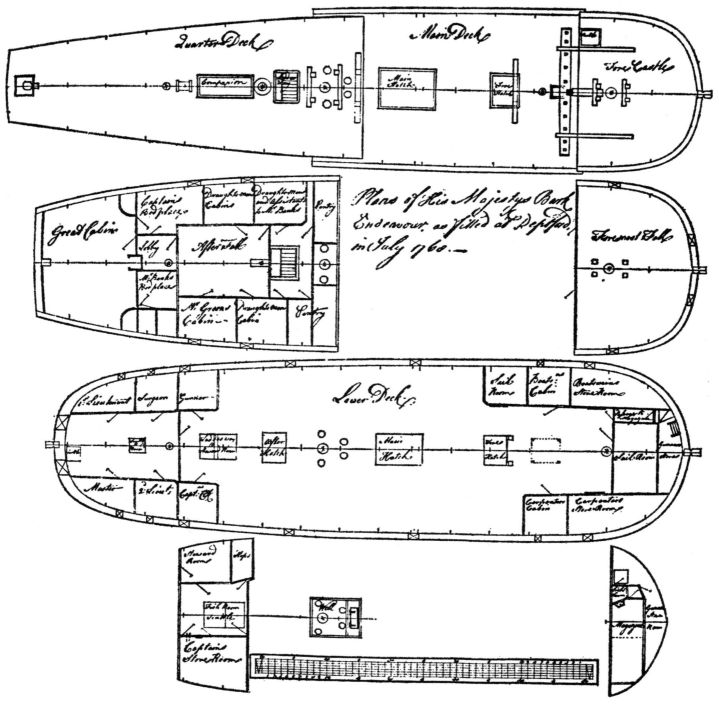

Deck plans of the *Endeavour* (National Maritime Museum, Greenwich).

it; possibly it had something to do with the fanciful and generally unpopular views he held regarding feeding his men with fresh foodstuffs.

Just when and where Cook was informed that he had been selected for command remains obscure. But in March 1768, the Navy Board, which was not celebrated for imaginative or original thinking, wrote the Admiralty a letter in such sensible terms that one suspects its officials must already have enjoyed at least an informative discussion with Cook himself. Their Lordships, suggested the Board, might care to consider a cat-built vessel (like a collier), which is "roomy and will afford the advantage of stowing and carrying a large quantity of provisions so necessary on such voyages, and in this respect preferable to a ship of war."

Matters were moving with unprecedented speed. Officials of the Navy Board sallied forth from their offices in Crutched Friars and began an inspection of several colliers then lying in the Thames. At the end of March, they bought the *Earl of Pembroke*.

The Navy promptly renamed her the *Endeavour*, but as there was already a fighting vessel of that name, they added the word "Bark," meaning in that sense a ship not designed for warfare at sea.

On 25 May 1768 James Cook was summoned to the Admiralty. He was handed his commission as lieutenant and formally instructed to take command of the *Endeavour* on her voyage round the world. He was then just forty years old. Two days later he opened his log with the words: "hoisted the pendant and took charge of the ship, she is lying in the basin in Deptford Yard."

The *Endeavour* was certainly no beauty. No contemporary plans or model of her exist, although a model made in more modern times, which is on display at the Royal Naval College, Greenwich, gives a very clear idea of her dimensions. The word "cat-built" is of Danish or Norwegian origin and was used to signify a ship of enormously strong construction, unusual stowage capacity, and shallow draught. The *Endeavour* was spacious, bluff-bowed, 105 feet in overall length, and a fraction over twenty feet in the beam. She had a square stern with a small windowed gallery off the captain's cabin. Fully laden, she would draw just over thirteen feet. A slow, ponderous, massive-beamed little vessel that could take an enormous amount of hard wear and buffeting, her sides and lower masts were protected with pine varnish, and her spars were painted black. Unlike Wallis' *Dolphin*, the *Endeavour* was not copper-bottomed to protect her from fast-sprouting marine growths and the destructive ravages of *teredos*, marine borer-worms; Cook was worried about repairing a metal sheathing if it were damaged by grazing coral heads or running aground. Nor had he any desire to clutter up the decks with a variety of cannon; the *Endeavour*'s total armament consisted of ten 4-pound guns, and twelve smaller swivel guns mounted on the open deck.

For two months the *Endeavour* lay beside the massive wooden wharf at Deptford while preparations were made for the voyage. The crew numbered eighty-three. Amongst them were a number o officers who had already crossed the South Pacific with Wallis. There were Robert Molyneux the master, John Gore a junior lieutenant, and the master's two mates, Pickersgill—an excellent hydrographer—and Clerke. Having savored the pleasures of Tahiti—a terrestrial paradise to men accustomed to the squalor of eighteenth-century England—all of them were eager to return there.

In addition to scientific stores such as botanists' tins, atlases, astronomical instruments, books, and charts, storage space had also to be found for ropes, sails, lumber, paints, spare rolls of canvas, and all the other items necessary for a long voyage. There were casks of biscuits, barrels of salted pork and beef, ponderous cheeses, and barrels of beer. The favorite food of British seamen was "burgoo" or "skillygolee," which consisted of a thin porridge with lumps of boiled meat floating in it. There was going to be plenty of it during the forthcoming voyage; the quantity of food available in British ships never caused any complaint. It was the quality that mattered, and the quality was bad.

The scurvy that killed off crews by the hundreds was caused by a deficiency of vitamin C, the vitamin found in fruit and vegetables. The East India Company suspected the truth of this fact and therefore made a habit of issuing its crews regular rations of fruit juice. Lind, a naval surgeon, was strongly recommending lime, lemon, or orange juice. But the Navy was slow to alter its ideas.

ENDEAVOUR

OBSERVATIONS of the Qualities, of His Majesty's ~~Ship~~ the *Endeavour*

r beſt Sailing Draft of Water, when victualed and ſtored for Channel Service, { Afore *13 - 6* } or as much lighter (at the ſame Difference) as ſhe is able to bear Sail
cing given this *3* — - Day of *Augſt* - - — *1771* - - - - { Abaft *13 - 10* }
~~r loweſt Gundeck-Port will then be above the Surface of the Water~~ — - —, or more

	In a Top Gallant Gale			Steers well and runs about 8 Knots —
	In a Topſail Gale			Six Knots
		{ How ſhe Steers, and how ſhe Wears and Stays }		Steers and Wears very Well
the 1ſt { How ſhe behaves close haul'd and how many Knots ſhe runs }	Under her	Reef Topſails		Reef her Topſails and she goes as Well as With Whole Topsails —
		Courses		She behaves as Well under her Courses as most Ships —
	And Query, Whether ſhe will ſtay under her Courſes			I do not remember that this was every tried —

2d. { In each Circumſtance above-mentioned (in Sailing with other Ships) in what Proportion ſhe gathers to Windward, and in what Proportion ſhe forereaches, and in general her Proportion of Lee-way. } — We never but once had an opportunity to try her With other Ships and then she fell to Leward, her proportion of Lee-way is a Point or a Point and a half

3d. { How ſhe proves in Sailing thro' all the Variations of the Wind from its being a Point or two Abaft the Beam, to its veering forward upon the Bow-line in every Strength of Gale, eſpecially in a ſtiff Gale and a head Sea; and how many Knots ſhe runs in each Circumſtance; and how ſhe carries her Helm. } — Her best Sailing is With the Wind a point or two abaft the beam she will then run 7 or 8 Knots and carry a Weather Helm —

4th. The moſt Knots ſhe runs before the Wind; and how ſhe Rolls in the Trough of the Sea. — Eight Knots, and Rolls easy in the Trough of the Sea —

5th. How ſhe behaves in lying Too or a Try, under a Main-ſail, and alſo under a Mizon ballanc'd. — No Sea can hurt her laying Too under a Main Sail or Mizon ballanced —

6th. What for a Roader ſhe is, and how ſhe Careens? — — — — She is a good Roader and Careens easy and without the least danger

7th. { If upon Trial the beſt ſailing Draft of Water given as above ſhould not prove to be ſo, what is the beſt ſailing Draft of Water? } — { Afore — Abaft — } Ft. Ins. As above

8th. What is her Draft of Water when victualed to ſix Months, and ſtored for Foreign Service? — Afore — *14 - 8* / Abaft — *15 - 0*

9th. What Height is her loweſt Gundeck-Port then above the Surface of the Water? — Under Water

10th. The Trim of the Ship. — — — — — — — Three or four Inches by the Stern —

Jamſ Cook

Cook's report to the Admiralty on the sailing qualities of the *Endeavour* (Public Record Office, London).

Cook's report on the state and condition of the *Endeavour* in July, 1771 (Public Record Office, London).

A Mr. Pelham of the Victualling Board also had some original thoughts of his own on the matter, so due to his efforts the *Endeavour*'s cargo included evaporated malt ("wort"), and pickled cabbage ("sauerkraut"). On his own initiative, Cook also obtained an extra large issue of vinegar. He knew by experience that scurvy flourished in living quarters that were damp, dark, and unhealthy. He was determined that vinegar and water would be used frequently to scrub out the crew's quarters aboard the ship, that the men would observe a high standard of hygiene, and that—whether they liked it or not, which they didn't—they would be forced to consume wort and sauerkraut at regular intervals.

With seventy-one officers and sailors aboard, the *Endeavour*'s accommodation was pretty full. But in addition there now came aboard twelve reluctant Marines. They wore high white gaiters, bright red tunics, and black leather ammunition pouches. A long bayonet dangled by each man's side, and his Tower musket was almost as tall as the man himself. These Marines would, of course, be quite useless in the ordinary routine of shipboard life; Cook, had he been given a choice, would probably have left them behind.

As passengers—there were eleven of them—there now came Mr. Charles Green of Greenwich Observatory and his assistants, all of whom had been nominated by the Royal Society. There was also the party belonging to that stalwart young amateur botanist Mr. Joseph Banks (later Sir Joseph Banks). Being extremely wealthy and of distinguished family, Banks had managed to persuade the authorities to allow him to accompany the *Endeavour*. In his party, and at his own expense, were Dr. Solander, a distinguished botanist, with Alexander Buchan and Sydney Parkinson to sketch the scenery and draw the plants. Also with this party were two Negro servants.

On 30 July 1768 the *Endeavour* sailed for Plymouth, where Banks and his party came aboard. At 2:00 P.M. on 26 August, crowded and heavily burdened, the little ship at last put out to sea, and thus began her three-year voyage. On board were "94 persons, including Officers, Seamen, Gentlemen and their Servants."

What Elizabeth Cook, now the mother of three small children, thought about it all, no one troubled to find out. She was probably wondering how much she would be able to save out of the five shillings per day the Navy was paying her husband. With a fourth child already on the way, the next few years looked like busy ones for her husband and herself.

The Admiralty instructions given to Cook were divided into two parts. In the first part, drawn up after consultation with the Royal Society, Lieutenant Cook was ordered to make his way via Cape Horn to King George's Island (Tahiti). He was to reach that island not later than one month before 3 June 1769, the date of the transit.

"When this service is performed you are to put to sea without loss of time, and carry into execution the Additional Instructions contained in the enclosed sealed packet."

These instructions, although secret at the time, remained so for 160 years afterwards, merely because no one ever got round to publishing them. They were at length discovered and published by the Navy Records Society in 1928.

"Whereas there is reason to believe that a Continent or Land of great extent may be found to the Southward of the Tract lately made by Captn Wallis in His Majesty's Ship the Dolphin... You are to proceed to the southward in order to make discovery of the Continent above-mentioned until you arrive in the Latitude of 40°, unless you sooner fall in with it. But not having discover'd it or any Evident signs of it in that Run, you are to proceed in search of it to the Westward between the Latitude before mentioned and the Latitude of 35° until you discover it, or fall in with

the Eastern side of the Land discover'd by Tasman and now called New Zealand."

There were many more instructions as to what he should do in the event he discovered new territories. He was to survey them, take possession ("with the Consent of the Natives") of Convenient Situations in the Country in the name of the King of Great Britain, note the magnetic deviation of the compass needle, collect samples of vegetation and minerals and observe the customs and manners of the native peoples. Having carried out all these tasks, Cook was free to make the choice as to whether he should make his return voyage to England via Cape Horn or the Cape of Good Hope.

For some strange reason, the Admiralty instructions contained no reference to Australia. They simply omitted the largest and most valuable territory in that part of the South Pacific across which Cook was to sail. Yet even in that year of 1769 more was known of Australia than of that mysterious land of New Zealand, sighted by Tasman 126 years earlier. It was up to Cook himself, who certainly must have noticed the omission, to rectify it in his own competent manner.

3 *"They led us to their meeting house."*
A carved lintel at the entrance to a Maori assembly house, showing a Clan Mother motif. The eyes are inlaid with glittering shell from the abalone, or haliotis mollusk (Auckland Museum, New Zealand).

4 *"He seemed to be chief. Round his neck was hanging a piece of green talk [sic], flat, and carved into the figure of a most uncooth animal of fancy."*
A Maori chief. He wears round his neck a jade ornament representing a Maori god. These carvings are the work of many months. Especially artistic pieces are preserved in the families of chiefs as precious heirlooms.

5 *"Many of the old and some of the middle aged men have their faces tatow'd with black figures."*
Mummified head of a Maori ancestor (Hooper Collection).

6 *"I had now seen enough of this passage to convence me that there was the greatest probabillty in the world on its runing into the Eastern Sea."*
Cook Strait, dividing the North Island from the South Island of New Zealand.

7 *"This house was well made. Over the doorway and at both sides were carved boards."*
Panel at the entrance to a Maori storehouse, originally from the Bay of Plenty, showing the popular theme of two lovers (Auckland Museum, New Zealand).

8 *"They wear a piece of Cloth wraped round their Middle and some thing over their Shoulders in which they carry their Children."*
Maori woman with a child.

9 *"Their Canoes are large well built and ornamented with carved work."*
Maori war canoe, drawn by Sydney Parkinson, who accompanied Cook on this voyage.

10 *"Their skilfull woodcarvings are to be seen on all things of their daily use."*
Maori houses and canoe. Each boat often carries a carved figure representing one of their gods (Auckland Museum, New Zealand).

11 *"There was a house built on piles."*
A Maori storehouse, richly ornamented with woodcarvings and protected by figures with protruding tongues as a sign of defiance.

12–14 *"I saw that we were surrounded on every side with Shoals and no such thing as a passage to Sea but through the winding channels between them, dangerous to the highest degree."*
(12) The Barrier Reef along the northeast coast of Australia. Cook's chartings during his voyages were of such enormous importance for all navigating nations that his charts were immediately copied and translated into other languages. Our plate shows a French one, published in Paris, 1778.
(13) The *Endeavour* at sea. Pencil drawing by Sydney Parkinson (British Museum).
(14) Within dangerous reefs.

15 *"I saw some trees that had been cut down by the natives with some sort of a blunt instrument and several trees that were barked the bark of which had been cut by the same Instrument."*
Maori bark painting (Auckland Museum, New Zealand). The New Zealand aborigines decorate the inside of their huts with pieces of bark on which they paint various things such as animals, human figures, scenes of their lives, or funeral ceremonies.

4

5

7

8

9

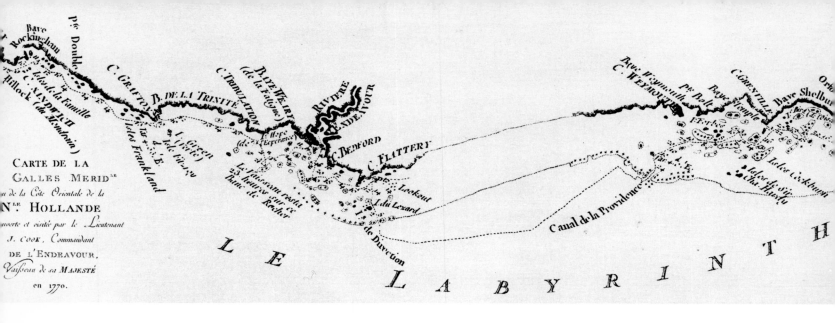

CARTE DE LA
GALLES MERID.^{LE}
u de la Côte Orientale de la
N.^{LE} HOLLANDE
uverte et visitée par le Lieutenant
J. COOK, Commandant
DE L'ENDEAVOUR.
Vaisseau de sa MAJESTÉ
en 1770.

LE LABYRINTH

< 11

13   14

12

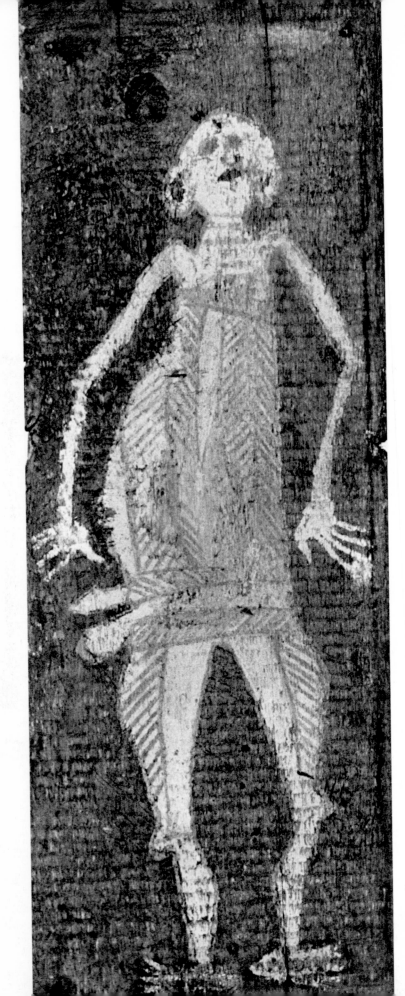

15

The Great Unknown

ith a badly leaking deck, seasick Marines and passengers, and great lumping green waves drowning the hens in their coops, the *Endeavour* plugged southward to Rio de Janeiro. During the spell of bad weather a lasting friendship began between Cook and the passenger about whom he was most worried, the twenty-five-year-old Joseph Banks.

There was nothing in common, or so it seemed, between this wealthy young aristocrat and the obscure naval officer in command of the little vessel. Yet while the *Endeavour* labored through the eighteen-foot rollers of the Bay of Biscay, Banks suddenly emerged on deck and began to climb unhandily up the mainmast to rescue two drenched and exhausted seabirds which had taken refuge there. On his way back to shelter below deck, Banks caught Cook's eye. Each man smiled at the other. A link had been established between them. Both were kind-hearted, both were prepared to go out of their way to prevent unnecessary suffering for any living creature.

After calling at Rio de Janeiro, where a Portuguese curmudgeon of a governor treated them with the greatest suspicion, the *Endeavour* continued her way toward Cape Horn. On 11 January 1769 she was off Tierra del Fuego, where Cook undertook some charting while Banks and the rest of the scientists landed to begin their botanical collections. Banks himself nearly lost his life while climbing a mountain in the company of Solander and the two Negro servants. A sudden snowstorm left them trapped on a ledge for hours, where the two Negro servants died of the cold. Solander would have suffered the same fate had it not been for Banks, who kept him marching along by the sheer physical force of a muscular arm.

The *Endeavour* was extremely lucky in spite of this minor disaster. So far on the voyage they had encountered nothing worse than the average weather to be expected in Atlantic waters. The short but highly dangerous stage of rounding the Cape proved much less of an ordeal than Cook and his more experienced officers had expected.

"Monday 13th February.
We are now advanced about 12° to the westward of the Strait of Magellan and 3¹/₂° to the Northward of it, having been 33 days in doubling Cape Horn or the land Terra del Fuego, and arriving into the degree of Latitude and Longitude we are now in without ever being brought once under our close reef'd Topsails since we left strait la Maire, a circumstance that perhaps never happened before to any ship in those Seas so much dreaded for Hard gales of Wind; in so much that the doubling of Cape Horn is thought by some to be a mighty thing, and others to this day prefer the Straits of Magellan. As I have never been in those Straits I can only form my Judgement on a Carefull Comparison of the Different Ships' Journals that have passed them, and those that have sail'd round Cape Horn, particularly the Dolphin's two last Voyages and this of ours, being made at the same season of the Year, when one may reasonably expect the same Winds to prevail. The Dolphin in her last Voyage was three months in getting through the Straits, not reckoning the time she lay in Port Famine; and I am firmly persuaded from the Winds we have had, that had we come by that Passage we should not have been in these Seas, besides the fatiguing of our People, the damage we must have done to our Anchors, Cables, Sails and Rigging, none of which have suffer'd in our passage round Cape Horn."

The Pacific Ocean gave the little ship and her crew a friendly welcome. It was the end of the hurricane season, which lasts from December to March, and the weather was settling down. In a latitude of 45° south, the southeast trade winds began to urge the little ship forward into warmer seas under a pleasantly blue sky. Passengers and crew alike gathered at the rails to gaze in wonder at the shoals of silvery-blue flying fish which scudded a foot or so above the surface of the sea, and a great playful dolphin gambolling ahead of the bows.

In early April, the *Endeavour* sighted several of the low palm-covered atolls or *motu* of the Tuamotu Archipelago, which to this day remain dangerous shoal and reef waters for vessels. Two days later, on 11 April 1769, the three-thousand-foot green peak of Tahiti's Mount Orohena came above the clear horizon, followed by the lower, bush-covered

First page of Cook's original journal of his first voyage (National Library, Canberra).

volcanic slopes and then—perhaps as a slight disappointment to the romantically minded Banks—the blackish sand of the beaches. While the ship sailed across a pleasantly ruffled sea, with the coast of Tahiti a few miles off the starboard bow, Cook sat at his desk in the great stern cabin to write in his log an entry that provides an interesting insight into the nature of that sturdy but tradition-bound fellow, the British seaman.

"Thursday 13th April.

At this time we had but a very few men upon the Sick list and these had but slight complaints, the Ships company had in general been very healthy owing in a great measure to the Sauerkraut, Portable Soup and Malt; the two first were serv'd to the People, the one on Beef Days and the other on Banyan Days, Wort was made of the Malt and at the discretion of the Surgeon given to every man that had the least symptoms of Scurvy upon him, by the Means and the care and Vigilance of Mr. Munkhous the Surgeon this disease was prevented from getting a footing in the Ship. The Sauerkraut the Men at first would not eate untill I put in practice a Method I never once knew to fail with seamen, and this was to have some of it dress'd every Day for the Cabin Table, and permitted all the Officers without exception to make use of it and left it to the option of the Men either to take as much as they pleased or none at all; but this practice was not continued above a week before I found it necessary to put every one on board to an Allowance, for such are the Tempers and dispositions of Seamen in general that whatever you give them out of the Common Way, altho it be ever so much for their good yet it will not go down with them and you will hear nothing but murmurings against the man that first invented it; but the Moment they see their Superiors set a Value upon it, it becomes the finest stuff in the World and the inventor an honest fellow."

In other words there is no use trying to reason with men who—like a majority of the modern Polynesians—are mentally incapable of reasoning in the Western way.

On the afternoon of that same day, 13 April, the *Endeavour* dropped anchor some two miles offshore in beautiful Matavai Bay on the northern coast of Tahiti.* Behind the palm-veiled foreshore, bluish-green peaks rose in bright splendor towards the tropical sky. Almost before the anchor spray had subsided, dozens of outrigger canoes, ranging in size from little craft with a single passenger to large ones carrying ten to fifteen islanders, were darting out from the shore.

At that time, the Tahitians were past their magnificent best as ocean navigators and warriors. Their way of life had always been more amoral than that of fellow-Polynesians on other islands, and just as the Romans declined in luxury and extreme sensuality, the Tahitians were beginning to do the same. They had ample land, ample food, and, by virtue of emigration to other more southerly islands, none of the pressing needs brought about by overpopulation.** In such conditions any race would probably decline, and the Polynesian, by virtue of his easy-going, indolent, and pleasure-loving nature, lapsed faster than most.

Samoa, a thousand miles to the west and peopled by a branch of the Polynesian race which was frequently at war with their Melanesian neighbors in the Fiji Islands, was already the rising new center of a hardier division of the race. In passing it might be mentioned that the Polynesians, who are of Europoid descent, originated in Asia and—as their own traditional chants and customs record—migrated eastward to Indo-China and ultimately reached the Pacific islands possibly during the era 300–400 A.D. Those who hold that the Polynesians originated in South America go—as one prominent ethnologist said—"to a great deal of trouble to prove something that never happened."

While the *Endeavour* lay at anchor, Cook and those officers who had visited the island with Wallis, accompanied by the indefatigable Banks, went ashore to choose a site for their astronomical observation. Left aboard the vessel, veteran seamen eyed approvingly the bare-breasted, brown-skinned girls in the canoes that were already bringing out welcome presents in the form of fish, fruit, coconuts, and yams, and undoubtedly wondered to themselves

---

* Which Cook and his contemporaries called Otaheite. Probably this inaccuracy was caused by a misunderstanding on the part of the Europeans. If spelt "O Tahiti" it would mean "of Tahiti," or "Tahitian." This was undoubtedly what the natives meant when answering questions from Cook and others regarding the island, the correct name of which is actually Tahiti-nui (Tahiti the Great).

** Infanticide was practiced to some extent to limit population.

how they would circumvent the captain's orders. Cook had made it very clear to the crew that all the natives were to be treated "with every imaginable humanity," that no officer or seaman should trade for any object he desired, and that no item of the ship's stores, particularly including iron or cloth, should be disposed of to win favor from the people.

While awaiting 3 June, the day on which the transit of Venus would take place, seamen and Tahitians intermingled on terms of intimate friendship. Too much so, according to Cook, who was greatly concerned over the spread of venereal disease amongst his crew. For this he blamed Bougainville's Frenchmen, on the dubious assumption that, as Wallis had made no mention in his log of the disease, at least during his own vessel's stay in Tahiti, it had not existed amongst the crew of the *Dolphin*. Quite rightly, Cook averred that it had been completely unknown in Tahiti before the advent of the white man. In an irate mood, he awarded two dozen lashes, the severest punishment of the voyage, to a seaman detected with much-coveted nails in his posession.

But this punishment was without avail. The defilement of seamen and Tahitians continued, while Banks with his classical education continued to bestow such nicknames as Hercules and Lycurgus on the handsome people and liken them to children in the Garden of Eden. He was not the first, nor by any means the last European, to make the same mistake, nor to discover that these apparently simple, laughing people were, very excusably, the most incredibly expert thieves. They already knew a little about iron. One of Roggeveen's ships had been wrecked in the Tuamotus in 1722, and a spike nail had been washed ashore. The story of it had spread.

"*Saturday 3rd June.*

This day prov'd as favourable to our purpose as we could wish, not a cloud to be seen the whole day and the Air was perfectly clear, so that we had every advantage we could desire in Observing the whole of the passage of the Planet Venus over the Suns disk; we very distinctly saw an Atmosphere or dusky shade round the body of the Planet which very much disturbed the times of the Contacts particularly the two internal ones. Dr. Solander observed as well as Mr. Green and myself, and we differ'd from one another in observeing the times of the Contacts much more than could be expected. Mr. Green's Telescope and mine were of the same Mag[n]ifying power but that of the Dr. was greater than ours. It was ne[a]rly calm the whole day and the Thermometer expos'd to the Sun about the middle of the Day rose to a degree of heat [119] we have not before met with."

It was unfortunate that observations taken in other parts of the world were unsuccessful, so nothing came of those by Cook at Fort Venus in Tahiti.

The *Endeavour* was careened during the second half of June and her underwater hull given a fresh coat of paint. Cook was now anxious to be gone, for a great many of his crew, to be precise twenty-four seamen and nine Marines, had developed symptoms of venereal disease.

It was certainly time for him to depart. A midshipman named James Matra had tried to organize a mass desertion by the other junior officers. Two Marines, Webb and Gibson, actually succeeded in doing so and took to the mountains with their female escorts. They were captured and brought back to the ship by Lieutenant Zachary Hicks.

The *Endeavour* left Tahiti in the middle of July, with most of the crew at least slightly disillusioned about the Eden-like qualities of the inhabitants. Behind them they left Alexander Buchan, who had died shortly after reaching the island.

No doubt the Tahitians themselves were also feeling somewhat disillusioned as to the godlike qualities of their white visitors. One of their menfolk had been shot dead by a Marine when attempting a particularly impudent theft. In spite of all the friendship demonstrated by both sides, bad-tempered and spiteful incidents had occurred. There was also the question of "the pox," as Surgeon Monkhouse called it, which was rapidly becoming prevalent amongst the people. Whether it was venereal disease still remains debatable, but modern medical opinion is inclined to believe that in some cases it was not. Yaws, deep oval sores with crater-like edges, was particularly common amongst the islanders and also highly contagious. No doubt some of Cook's seamen were infected by personal contact. At any rate, the sores began to heal up after the ship left Tahiti and none of the sailors suffered any ill effects. Or so it was said at the time. The fact remains that in Polynesian tradition, those first three European captains, Wallis, Bougainville, and Cook, are blamed for having introduced venereal disease to the island.

Throughout Polynesia at that time the great sea-god of the people was variously known as Tangaroa or Ta'aroa, depending on the local dialect. All legends of this god agree that he was fair-haired, white-skinned, and possibly blue-eyed. It was said that Tangaroa guided the first migratory canoes of the Polynesians during the period of their gradual and centuries-long migration eastward across the Pacific to the islands. Ancient chants in his honor are still occasionally performed in modern times. It was only natural, therefore, that the first white visitors to Tahiti, and later to other islands, should be accepted as the direct descendants of this god. Throughout the western Pacific, where, it could be suggested, the Polynesians had not relied on the services of Tangaroa as a navigator of their ocean-voyaging canoes, his name, although known, was not venerated to the same extent as in Tahiti, Rarotonga, and Hawaii.

One fact must be obvious: after the visit of three European ships to Tahiti, not even the most optimistic *taunga* (priest) could continue to ascribe godlike qualities to eighteenth-century seamen.

For three weeks the *Endeavour* cruised among the islands to the northwest of Tahiti, discovering the fertile Leeward Group in the process. Then, with his thoughts on the calendar, Cook swung southwest to begin the quest for *Terra Australis*.

The weather was unpleasant for most of the voyage. The Journal refers frequently to "very strong gales with heavy squalls of wind, hail and

Tahitian double-canoe. Pencil drawing by H. D. Spöring, who accompanied Cook on one of his voyages (British Museum).

rain." A long, deep swell from the westward indicated that it was unlikely there was any land in that direction for a long way. Nor was there any sign of land at other points of the compass. The swinging flight of an occasional albatross or a fast-winged stormy petrel were the only signs of life across this grey, endless horizon of ocean.

On Saturday, 7 October, a day of gentle breezes and settled weather, land was sighted in latitude 38° 57′ south. This point was an arm of Poverty Bay near the middle of the eastern coast of New Zealand.

On 9 October Cook, accompanied by Banks and Solander, Tupia, the interpreter they had brought from Tahiti, and a number of seamen, landed close to the mouth of a river on this unknown coast.

"Seeing some of the natives on the other side of the river whom I was desirous of speaking with and finding that we could not ford the river, I order'd the yawl in to carry us over and the Pinnace to lay at the entrance. In the mean time the Indians made off; however we went as far as their hutts which lay about 2 or 3 hundred yards from the water side, leaving four boys to take care of the yawl, which we had no sooner left than four men came out of the woods on the other side of the river and would certainly have cut her off, had not the people in the pinnace discover'd them, and called to her to drop down the stream which they did, being closely pursued by the Indians; the Coxwain of the pinnace who had the charge of the Boats, seeing this fir'd two musquets over their heads, the first made them stop and look round them, but the 2nd they took no notice of upon which a third was fired and killed one of them upon the spot just as he was going to dart his spear at the boat; at this the other three stood motionless for a minute or two, seemingly quite surprised [and] wondering no doubt what it was that had thus killed their comrade; but as soon as they recover'd themselves they made off draging the dead body a little way and then left it."

The New Zealand Maori was a very different type of fellow from the sun-bathed, easy-going Polynesian of Tahiti. Although the Maori had emigrated in large numbers to New Zealand from eastern Polynesia during a series of voyages made, according to native legends and modern research, over the thirteenth and fourteenth centuries, the colder, harder country had greatly altered his nature. He had become heavier, more robust, an ardent cannibal, and generally much more bloodthirsty. Probably his blood had become mixed in the land of his adoption with that of primitive Melanesian voyagers —drift or otherwise—who had also arrived on the coasts of New Zealand. The Maori of the eighteenth century had retained many of the traditional skills of his homeland and even improved on them in a number of directions. He was highly intelligent, even gifted at times, but with much less inclination than his Polynesian brothers to love, laugh, and play. He was also much less inclined to keep himself and was very appreciably darker-skinned. His was not the temperament to welcome unknown white-skinned strangers to his shores.

"Tuesday 10th October.
PM. I rowed round the head of the Bay but could find no place to land, on account of the great surf which beat every where upon the shore; seeing two boats or Canoes coming in from Sea, I rowed to one of them in order to seize upon the people and came so near before they took notice of us that Tupia called to them to come along side and we would not hurt them, but instead of doing this they endeavoured to get away, upon which I order'd a Musquet to be fired over their heads thinking that this would either make them surrender or jump over board, but here I was mistaken for they immediately took to their arms, or whatever they had in the boat, and began to attack us, this obliged us to fire upon them and unfortunately either two or three were kill'd, and one wounded, and three jumped over board, these last we took up and brought on board, where they were clothed and treated with all imaginable kindness and to the surprise of every body became at once as cheerful and as merry as if they had been with their own friends; they were all three young, the eldest not above 20 years of age and the youngest about 10 or 12.
"I am aware that most humane men who have not experienced things of this nature will censure my conduct in firing upon the people in this boat nor do I myself think that the reason I had for seizing upon her will at all justify me, and had I thought that they would have made the least resistance I would not have come near them, but as they did I was not to stand still and suffer either my self or those that were with me to be knocked on the head."

Cook began to prepare an accurate chart of the prominent landmarks of the coast and its general trend. Sailing northward, he rounded Cape Maria

43

CAPTIONS OF PLATES 16–30

16 *"On a board inside this house there was a monstrous looking sort of head dress with human hairs."*
Tahitian ceremonial mask (British Museum).

17–21 *"They said, that their god came and fed upon the sacrifices. Upon its being objected, that they prevented his feeding on the human victim, by burying him, they answered, that he fed only on the soul."*
"Those who are devoted to suffer, in order to perform this bloody act of worship, are guilty persons and are never apprized of their fate, till the blow is given that puts an end to their existence."
"The morai is undoubtedly a place of worship, sacrifice, and burial, at the same time. At the entrance there are two figures with human faces. Its principal part, is a large, oblong pile of stones, lying loosely upon each other, under which the bones of the Chiefs are buried."
"There are several reliquiae scattered about this place; such as small stones, some with bits of cloth tied round them; and a great many pieces of carved wood and figures."
Marae Attahooroo at Tahiti, where Cook witnessed the ceremonies of a human sacrifice, to implore the assistance of the Tahitian god of war against the neighboring island Eimeo.

22, 23 *"They are almost black or rather of a dark Chocolate Colour, and have Wolly hair."*
"They in general are tall, well shaped and some are almost as fair as Europeans. Their hair they let grow long and hang loose over their shoulders."
The natives of the South Sea islands show a racial mixture that ranges from a near-Caucasian appearance to Negroid.
(22) A typical Melanesian islander of Negroid appearance.
(23) Omai, the fair-looking Polynesian brought from Tahiti to England on Cook's second voyage, according to an engraving of 1778.

24 *"The fan, or fly-flap, is also an ornament used by both sexes. The most valuable are those which have the handle made of the arm or leg bones of an enemy slain in battle, and which are preserved with great care, and handed down, from father to son, as trophies of inestimable value."*
Carved handle of a fly whisk from Tahiti, representing two squatting figures joined back to back. Fly whisks probably were also used during religious ceremonies (Hooper Collection).

25 *"In the afternoon he and the whole Royal Family made me a Viset on board; His Father made me a present of a compleat Mourning dress."*
Mourning dress of Tahitian chiefs (British Museum).

26 *"In order to prevent them from overseting when in the water all those that go single both great and small have what is call'd outriggers which are peices of wood fasten'd to the gunel and project out on one side about 6, 8 or 10 feet according to the size of the boat."*
Outrigger canoe in a bay of Moorea, one of the Society Islands. Outriggers were only used for coasting; distant voyages were undertaken in double-canoes.

27–29 *"The Island of Bolabola is incompass'd by a Reef of rocks and several small Islands. This Island is very remarkable on account of a high craggy hill upon it, which terminates at top in two peeks the one higher than the other. Yet the Hills looks green and pleasant and are in many places Cloath'd with woods."*
(27) Evening twilight at Bora Bora in the Society Islands, one of the most beautiful islands in the Pacific Ocean.
(28) Mount Pahia at Bora Bora.
(29) Spur of Mt. Pahia, with a distant coral reef and lagoon.

30 *"This Harbour taken in its greatest extent is capable of holding any number of Shipping in perfect security as it extends almost the whole length of this side of the Island and is defended from the sea by a reef of Coral rocks, the southermost opening in this reef or Channell into the Harbour is not more then a Cables length wide."*
Taputapuatea, the most sacred marae of all Polynesia stood at the harbor of Opoa on Raiatea in the Society Islands.

20   21

22

23

24

25

29

Van Dieman, so named by Tasman, before the close of the year 1769. The *Endeavour* then went south along the western coast charted by Tasman until he reached the great channel dividing North from South Island.

Tasman had believed that this gulf was merely a bay, but now Cook disproved this theory by sailing right through it, an accomplishment noted by the name of Cook Strait which it bears today. In a sheltered bay on the northern coast of South Island, which he named Queen Charlotte Sound, the *Endeavour* was laid ashore and again careened. Fortunately for those concerned, the Maori in this district proved reasonably lukewarm in their friendship and apart from hurling stones every now and then, they never displayed the insatiable ferocity of their northern neighbors.

In February 1770 Cook sailed northward from this hospitable cove until he again reached Cape Turnagain, the point which he had first reached after sighting New Zealand. Thereafter he turned south to investigate the rest of the land lying south of Cook Strait.

Heavy rain and high seas made the *Endeavour*'s charting of the coast a difficult matter. No one could blame Cook for mistaking Banks Peninsula as an island, nor for believing that Stewart Island at the southern tip of New Zealand was actually part of the mainland. Cloud wrack and more rain on the western coast of South Island also prevented him from sighting the snowy cap of what was later named Mount Cook (12,700 feet). He did not fail to note, however, the mountainous character of the country—mountains of a strange, volcanic appearance totally unlike anything in Europe but in formation at least somewhat resembling those of Tahiti.

"A ridge of mountains," wrote Cook, "of prodigious height which appear to consist of nothing but barren rocks, covered in many places with large patches of snow which appear to have lain there since creation. No country upon earth can appear with a more rugged and barren aspect than this doth."

To those eighteenth-century navigators, seamen, and scientists, only a fertile landscape was "beautiful." A soft and gentle countryside could be fenced, plowed, and farmed. It was Wordsworth who, in a later age, urged mankind to appreciate the natural beauty of mountain and forest. New Zealand's Southern Alps were superbly beautiful in their splendor of native forest, ferny bush, and high-peaked, tree-covered mountain sides. Cook was seeing them through the eyes of an earlier age.

The *Endeavour*'s sails were furled when her anchor splashed into the tranquil waters of Admiralty Bay, somewhat to the west of Queen Charlotte Bay. Tasman's own ship had anchored in that same sheltered inlet 128 years earlier.

In six months of strenuous survey work, Cook had charted the whole of the New Zealand coastline, a total length of twenty-four hundred miles. A French naval officer named de Surville who visited New Zealand two years later declared that Cook's chart, of which he possessed a copy, was "of an exactitude and of a thoroughness of detail which astonished me beyond all power of expression. I doubt whether our own coasts of France have been delineated with more precision." Under the date of 31 March 1770, a day or so before he quitted New Zealand, Cook prepared a most interesting and accurate account of the Maori of that country, a savage, cannibal yet attractive and picturesque people.

"The natives of this country are a strong, raw-boned well-made, Active people rather above than under the common size especially the men, they are all of a very dark brown Colour with black hair, thin black beards and white teeth, and such as do not disfigure their faces by tattooing &ca. have in general very good features. The men generally wear their hair long, combed up and tied upon the crown of their heads; some of the women wear it long and loose upon their shoulders, old women especially; others again wear it crop'd short: their combs are some made of bone and others of wood, they sometimes wear them as an ornament stuck upright in their hair. They seem to enjoy a good state of health and many of them live to a good old age. Many of the old and some of the middle-aged men have their faces mark'd or tattoo'd with black and some few we have seen who have their buttocks, thighs and other parts of their bodies mark'd but this is less common.

"One day... I saw a strong proof that the women never appear naked at least before strangers. Some of us happen'd to land upon a small Island where several of them were naked in the water gathering Lobsters and Shell fish. As soon as they saw us, some of them hid themselves among the rocks and the rest remain'd in the Sea until they had made themselves aprons of the Sea weed and even then when they came out to us they shew'd manifest signs of Shame and those who had no method of hiding their nakedness would by no means appear before us. The making of Cloth and all other Domestic work is, I believe, wholly done by them and the more labourous work such as build Boats, Houses, Tilling the ground, fishing &ca. by the Men. Both men and women wear ornaments at their ears and about their necks. These are made of Stone, bone, Shells &ca. and are variously shaped, and some I have seen wear human teeth and finger nails, and I think we were told that they did belong to their deceas'd friends. The men when they are dress'd generally wear two or three long white feathers stuck upright in their hair, and at Queen Charlotte's Sound many both men and women wore round Caps made of black feathers"....

"Whenever we were visited by any number of them that had never heard or seen anything of us before, they generally came off in the largest Canoes they had, some of which will carry 60, 80 or 100 people, they always brought their best clothes along with them which they put on as soon as they came near the Ship. In each Canoe were generally an Old man, in some two or three, these use'd always to direct the others, were better Clothed and generally carried a halberd or battle ax in their hands or some such like thing that distinguished them from the others. As soon as they came within about a stone's throw of the Ship they would there lay and call out *Haromai Hareuta a patoo age** that is come here, come ashore with us and we will kill you with our patoo's***, and at the same, would shake them at us, at times they would dance the war dance, and other times they would trade with and talk to us, and answer such questions as were put to them with all the Calmness imaginable, and then again begin the war dance... Musketry they never regarded unless they felt the effect, but great guns they did because these threw stones farther than they could comprehend. After they found that our Arms were so much superior to theirs and that we took no advantage of that superiority, and a little time given them to reflect upon it, they ever after were our very good friends and we never had an instance of their attempting to surprise or cut off any of our people when they were ashore, opportunities for so doing they must have had at one time or another."

* *Haeremai, haere ki uta; ka patu iakoe.* RS.
** *Patu:* short-handled stone fighting-axe. RS.

SHIPWRECK

ook had now carried out his orders and could consider himself free to return to England by any route he chose. It was his intention to round Cape Horn again in order to prove or disprove beyond all trace of doubt that the alleged southern continent did not exist. Banks, who had formerly believed in Dalrymple's hypothesis, was already quite convinced of "the total destruction of our aerial fabric called Continent," but Cook guessed rightly that the tiresome Dalrymple would be much harder to convince. However, he had to face the fact that the *Endeavour* was no longer in a state for a voyage in high latitudes. He decided therefore to return to England by the Cape of Good Hope, after refitting in the East Indies. On its way to Batavia in Java, it would be possible for the *Endeavour* to take a long look at the unknown eastern coast of New Holland (Australia) and ascertain the exact whereabouts of Torres Strait. Generations of Dutch captains had charted the western coast of Australia, the southern coast for half its length, and the northern coast to a more considerable distance, including the Gulf of Carpentaria. No European was known to have sighted the eastern coast which some hydrographers believed to be continuous with that of New Guinea.

The *Endeavour* sailed from New Zealand on 1 April 1770. If Cook had been able to maintain the course he proposed to steer, he would have sighted Tasmania and continued the discovery of its coastline at the point where Tasman had left it. But as the *Endeavour* neared the land, she was forced to make headway through a violent southwesterly gale which forced her onto a more northerly course. It was not until 1798 that later explorers finally proved Tasmania to be an island.

For more than a week the *Endeavour* followed the new coast northwards, a grey, low-lying but rocky and dangerous coast, without finding an inlet through which boats could reach the shore without grave risk of being capsized in the monstrous surf. On 28 April, however, a generous entrance was noticed, ultimately to be named Botany Bay, a few miles south of modern Sydney. At daylight the following morning, after the pinnace had carried out careful soundings, Cook took the *Endeavour* into the bay.

This was a strange country. It was devoid of the fragrant foliage of beautiful Tahiti; it lacked the splendid forests, snow-capped mountains, and wide green river flats of New Zealand. It was a silent, dry, brooding expanse of nothingness, vast in area and utterly lacking in charm and personality. The apathetic natives were completely different from the active, vigorous inhabitants of New Zealand. Even the clumsy logs they used as canoes were nothing compared with the long, graceful and entirely seaworthy canoes of the Tahitians, or the heavier, highly-decorated craft of the New Zealand Maori.

"Sunday 29th April.
Saw as we came in on both points of the bay Several of the natives and a few hutts, Men, women and children on the south shore abreast of the Ship, to which place I went in the boats in hopes of speaking with them, accompanied by Mr. Banks, Dr. Solander and Tupia; as we approached the shore they all made off except two Men who seemed resolved to oppose our landing. As soon as I saw this I ordered the boats to lay upon their oars in order to speak to them, but this was to little purpose for neither us nor Tupia could understand one word they said. We then threw them some nails beads &ca. ashore which they took up and seem'd not ill pleased in so much that I thought that they beckon'd to us to come ashore; but in this we were mistaken, for as soon as we put the boat in, they again came to oppose us, upon which I fired a musket between the two which had no other effect than to make them retire back where bundles of their darts lay, and one of them took up a stone and threw at us which caused my fireing a second Musquet load with small shott, and altho some of the shott struck the man, yet it had no other effect than to make him lay hold of a Shield or target to defend himself. Immediately after this we landed which we had no sooner done than they threw two darts at us, this obliged me to fire a third shott soon after which they both made off, but not in such haste but what we might have taken one, but Mr. Banks being of the opinion that the darts were poisoned, made me cautious how I advanced into the woods. We found here a few small hutts made of the bark of trees in one of which

were four or five small children with whom we left some strings of beeds &ca. A quantity of darts lay about the hutts, these we took away with us. Three Canoes lay upon the bea[c]h the worst I think I ever saw they were about 12 or 14 feet long made of one piece of the bark of a tree drawn or tied up at each end and the middle kept open by means of pieces of sticks by way of Thwarts."

Seaman Torby Sutherland was buried ashore on 1 May, "at the watering place which occasioned my calling the south point of this Bay after his name."

The name first given to Botany Bay by Cook was the much less attractive one of Stingray Harbour, on account of the quantity of that unpleasant fish they found there. It was only on learning from Banks and Solander that the place contained a remarkable number of unknown flowers that Cook made the alteration. At this point, his usually accurate judgment seems to have gone astray in this desolate inlet. Possibly the responsibilities of the voyage were beginning to weigh heavily on him, and he may have been suffering from the mental fatigue caused by endless hours spent over the new charts he had prepared. The sandy soil must have indicated to him that the land would be useless for agricultural purposes, and the rapidly shoaling waters near the shore indicated equally clearly that the place was unlikely to prove a good berth for future ships. Yet he left on record an impression that he considered the place quite suitable for cultivation and made mention of a "rich meadow" in the locality, of "a very fine stream of fresh water," and a cove in which "a Ship might lay almost landlock'd and wood for fuel may be got everywhere."

The *Endeavour* spent a week at Botany Bay. She left on 7 May to sail rapidly onwards up the coast, naming—but not entering—Port Jackson on the way.

Difficulties now began to threaten the little ship. The coastline was becoming dangerous with shoals. Far out to sea, at a distance varying from one hundred to two hundred miles, the southern end of the Great Barrier Reef, a mass of sharp-edged coral formation rising steeply from the depths of the ocean, ran northwestward towards the Torres Strait, converging steadily on the mainland the further northward it went.

The *Endeavour* was sailing through the dangerous waters between the eastern coast of Australia and the Reef, a fact completely unknown to Cook at the time.

On the evening of 11 June the presence of low-lying islands and wave-washed rocks warned Cook that he was entering a perilous stretch of sea.

"At this time I had everybody at their stations to put about and come to anchor but in this I was not so fortunate for meeting again with deep water I thought there could be no danger in standing on. Before 10 o'Clock we had 20 and 21 fathom and continued in that depth until a few Minutes before 11 when we had 17, and before the Man at the lead could heave another cast the Ship struck and stuck fast. Immediately upon this we took in all our sails, hoisted out the boats and sounded round the Ship, and found that we had got upon the SE edge of a reef of Coral rocks, having in some places round the Ship 3 and 4 fathom water and in other places not quite as many feet, and about a Ships length from us on our starboard side (the ship laying with head to the NE) were 8, 10 and 12 fathom . . . We not only started water but throw'd overboard our guns Iron and stone ballast Casks, Hoops, staves, oil Jars, decay'd stores &ca, many of these last articles lay in the way at coming at heavyer. All this time the Ship made little or no water. At 11 o'Clock in the AM being high-water as we thought we try'd to heave her off without success, she not being afloat by a foot or more, notwithstanding by this time we had thrown over board 40 or 50 Tun weight; as this was not found sufficient, we continued to Lighten her by every method we could think of. As the Tide fell the Ship began to make water as much as two Pumps could free. At Noon she lay with 3 or 4 Strakes heel to Starboard."

Coral is the most deadly type of rock on which a ship can pile aground. Of brittle substance, yet with jagged cutting edges and innumerable spurs, it allows the vessel to embed itself deeper with every surge of the waves. Even the normal rise and fall of the tide on a perfectly calm day, weather such as Cook experienced during this emergency, is sufficient for this embedding action to continue. On a wooden hull, the continued effect is deadly. The *Endeavour* was saved by the remarkably cool and expert seamanship of her disciplined crew.

Throughout the rest of that frightening day, 12 June, Cook and his men went on struggling to

65

free the ship. It was their only hope of escape. If they failed in their efforts they would be able to make the coast of the mainland in the boats, but what kind of existence awaited them there? They were thirteen thousand miles from home, no one else had any idea where they were, and even if they escaped being massacred by the aborigines, or dying of hunger and thirst, they would possibly spend the rest of their lives in this inhospitable country awaiting a rescue that never came. Discipline amongst even naval crews frequently broke down in the face of disaster, but on this occasion there was no sign of mutiny or even laxity amongst the men. They worked swiftly and obediently, punctiliously carrying out every order their commander gave them.

"Tuesday 12th June.

Fortunately we had little wind, fine weather and a smooth Sea all these 24 hours which in the PM gave us an opportunity to carry out the two bower Anchors, the one on the starboard quarter and the other right astern. Got blocks and tackles upon the Cables, brought the falls in abaft and hove taut. By this time it was 5 o'Clock in the pm, the tide we observed now began to rise and the leak increased upon us which obliged us to set the 3rd Pump to work as we should have done the 4th also, but could not make it work. At 9 o'Clock the Ship righted and the leak gaind upon the Pumps considerably. This was an alarming and I may say terrible Circumstance and threatened immediate destruction to us as the Ship was afloat. However I resolved to risk all and heave her off in case it was practical, and accordingly turnd as many hands to the Capstan and windlass as could be spared from the Pumps and about 20′ past 10 o'Clock the Ship floated and we hove her off into deep water having at this time 3 feet 9 inches water in the hold."

Cook saved his ship by carrying out a procedure which seafaring men had established during centuries of bitter experience. On striking a shoal, a ship's boats were always lowered to take soundings all round the obstruction to discover where the greatest depth of water existed. Anchors were then taken in the boats to this deeper water and lowered into position. The ship was lightened by throwing overboard everything that could be spared, and the capstan in the bow then began to heave taut

the cables attached to the sunken anchors. On this occasion Cook sacrificed some dubious stores, twenty-five tons of fresh water, three or four tons of firewood, several tons of stone and iron ballast, and six of the 12-pounder guns from the deck.

Once the *Endeavour* was afloat, Cook followed another expedient known to seafarers since the earliest times. He proceeded to "fother" the hull. This was done by filling an old canvas sail with oakum (stranded fiber made by unpicking rope), wool, and rags, and then passing it under the bow where the suction of the water swirling in through the leak forced it tightly against the damaged part of the underwater hull and held it in that position. The temporary expedient worked so well that the leak could be dealt with by a single pump instead of the three pumps that earlier had been barely adequate. The whole idea of "fothering" the *Endeavour* had been suggested to Cook by a midshipman named Monkhouse "who was once in a Merchant ship which sprung a leak and made 48 inches water per hour but by this means was brought home from Virginia to London... To him I gave the direction of this [fothering] who executed it very much to my satisfaction."

Slowly they made their way back to Endeavour River, a small creek or inlet not more than a mile long near the modern town of Cooktown. No ordinary merchant ship could have crossed the shallow bar at the entrance, but the shallow-draft collier was just able to pass over it. Once again Cook's choice of a vessel had been vindicated.

The vessel was brought in close to the beach so that when the tide fell the damage to her hull was exposed. There were several holes made by the coral and four planks neatly severed. One large block of coral was still tightly wedged in the cavity it had made. During the next six weeks, while the crew camped on shore, the carpenters made as sound a repair as possible. Even so, it was strongly advisable to sail the *Endeavour* to the nearest dockyard, which meant Batavia, in the shortest possible time.

When the ship was ready to put to sea again, Cook decided to steer eastward until he reached the open sea. He was thoroughly disgusted with constricted waters and coral heads that loomed up without warning from the depths.

In order to reach the ocean, he had to sail cautiously through a studded necklace of low-lying sandy islands on which grew nothing but a few small and windtwisted trees. But scarcely had he reached the sea when the wind dropped. A heavy swell and a flooding tide carried the vessel straight toward the outer coral heads of the reef, and it was only at the last moment, when a final tragedy threatened to wipe out the ship and drown the crew, that Cook caught sight of a small but deep inlet a few hundred yards away—Providence Channel he promptly christened it.

Hastily lowered boats managed to tow the *Endeavour* toward this swell-choked passage, and the ship was swept through it, temporarily out of control, like a piece of flotsam surging on the crest of an incoming roller.

The experience shook even Cook's indomitable nerve. It was the narrowest escape he ever encountered.

"It is but a few days ago that I rejoiced at having got without the reef," he wrote in his Journal, "but that joy was nothing to what I now felt at being safe at anchor within it."

Never again would he take a chance with the Great Barrier Reef. For better or worse, he decided to sail along the channel between it and the mainland.

On 21 August 1770 he thankfully reached the end of this dangerous east coast and sighted Cape York, its most northerly extremity. He bestowed the name New Wales on the two-thousand-mile coastline he had finished exploring, and took possession of it on behalf of Britain. (The present name, New South Wales, appears also in Cook's Journal. When Captain Matthew Flinders of the Royal Navy first circumnavigated the continent in 1803, he suggested that the name Australia should replace the old name of New Holland. This new name was officially approved in 1817. Cook himself never saw Australia again.)

Westward into the deep, safe waters of Torres Strait—so named by Dalrymple in honor of that intrepid Portuguese pilot who sailed through it in 1606—the *Endeavour* now began to hasten forward under full canvas. She entered Batavia Roads on 10 October.

Examination of her hull by shipwrights revealed that the damage was much more serious than even Cook had supposed. Repairs would take longer than expected, so for the next two months passengers and crew alike were exposed to one of the unhealthiest climates in the world.

There had not been a single case of sickness aboard the *Endeavour* when they reached Java, and only eight men had died during the entire voyage up to the present, none of them of scurvy. But now came malaria, dysentery, and God knows how many other types of tropical illness. After breathing pure air for nearly two years, Cook's men had little resistance to disease. Seven of them died in Batavia, amongst them Dr. Monkhouse, and poor Tupia, the Tahitian who had joined the ship with the ambition of seeing for himself the wonderful world of the *Popaa* (European).

Sickness accompanied the ship when she sailed for Capetown on 26 December. The *Endeavour's* crew went on dying, and amongst those to be buried at sea during the remainder of the voyage were Charles Green the astronomer, Sydney Parkinson, Lieutenant Hicks, and Robert Molyneux the master. Many other members of the crew, including Cook himself, were taken ill. The only seaman who completely escaped any kind of sickness was an ancient sailmaker, some seventy years old. "What is still more extraordinary in this man," wrote Cook, "is his generally being more or less drunk every day."

On 10 July 1771 Land's End was sighted from the *Endeavour's* masthead, and anchor was dropped two days later. The ship had been away from England for almost exactly three years. Thirty-eight of the ninety-four men who sailed in her had failed to return.

CAPTIONS OF PLATES 31–46

31 *"It is of a round form and hath deep water close to its shores. All the Sea Coast is wholy covered with Trees Shrubery."*
One of the uninhabited little coral islands surrounding New Caledonia.

32 *"Their Houses or at least the most of them are circular, the roof is high and peaked to a point at the top above which is a post or stick of wood which is generally ornamented with either carving or shells or both."*
Detail of the top of a New Caledonian house (Museum für Völkerkunde, Vienna).

33, 34 *"Here were, besides the Pines, a variety of other trees, Shrubs and Plants which gave sufficient employment to our botanists."*
Subtropical primeval forest on New Caledonia.

35 *"They make the same kind of Cloth and of the same materials as at Otaheite. Their Colours are all made from Vegetables. They make various sorts of Matting and some of a very fine texture, this is generally used for cloathing and the thick and strong sort is used to Sleep on and to make sails for their Canoes &ca."*
Tapa from the Tonga Islands, decorated with representations of the frigate bird. Tapa is a coarse cloth made by rasping and pounding the bark of the paper mulberry tree. The figures and ornamentation on it are painted on, or printed with various stamps, or stenciled in several colors.

36, 37 *"Their Ornaments are Amulets, Necklaces and Bracelets, of Bone Shells and beads of Mother of pearl, Tortise Shell &ca these are worn by both sex."*
Two small figures (male and female) from the Tonga Islands representing local deities, carved from whale ivory. Such figures were worn by the aborigines round the neck as amulets against disease. They are very rare and precious.
(36) John Hewett Collection.
(37) Museum für Völkerkunde, Vienna.

38 *"The Men had no other covering than the case to the Penis and a kind of Turband about the head, in which were stuck some long feathers."*
New Caledonian warriors in their dancing costumes.

39, 43, 44 *"Benevolent Nature has certainly been very bountifull to these isles."*
Views of the romantic landscape of the Tonga Islands.

40 *"I observed several old plantations laying in fallow, some pieces of which they were again beginning to dig up, the first thing they do is to set fire to the grass &ca which had over run its Surface."*
New Caledonia. To cultivate the land the natives first burn the luxuriant natural vegetation.

41 *"The well carved dish was garnished with hot bread fruit and Plantains."*
Wooden food vessel from the Admiralty Islands (Museum für Völkerkunde, Vienna).

42 *"The weapons, which they make, are clubs of different sorts (in the ornamenting of which they spend much time), spears, and darts."*
The typical war club of nearly all Oceanic islanders, made of a dark brown hardwood. The one shown here came from the Fiji Islands and is now at the Museum für Völkerkunde, Vienna.

45 *"They live chiefly by fishing, making use either of nets of different kinds, or of wooden fish-hooks pointed with bone."*
Fisherman's dwelling on the edge of a lagoon in the New Hebrides.

46 *"Having landed near some of their houses and Plantations which were just within the Skirts of the Woods, I prevaild on one men to let me see them. Their houses are low and covered with thick Palm thatch, their form is oblong and some are boarded at the ends where the entrance is by a Square Port hole."*
Small native settlement on New Caledonia.

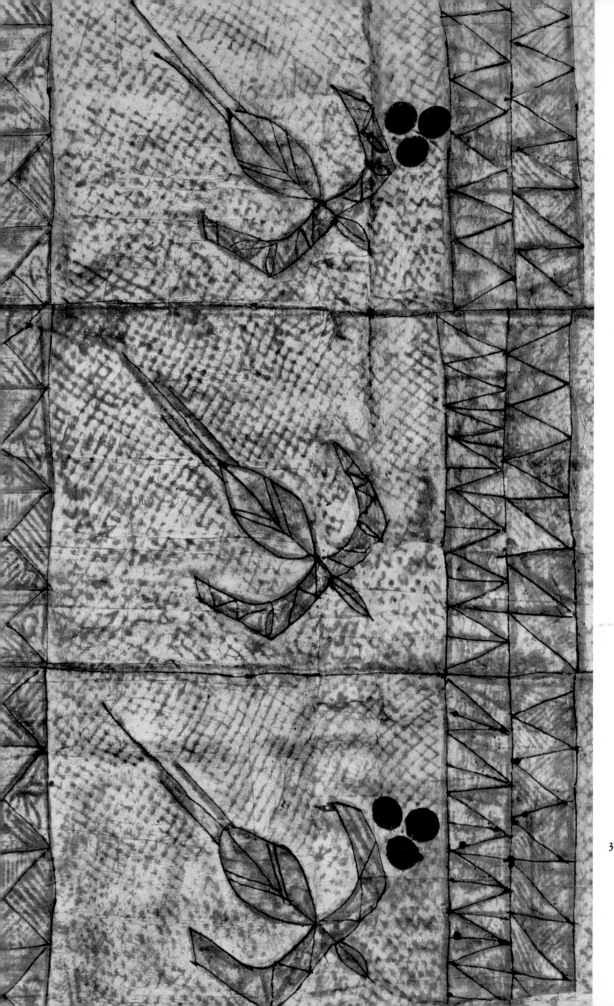

40

41

42

Second Voyage

ames Cook, the son of a laborer, had come a long way. Almost overnight he became a notable figure in rakish but brilliant London society, even to the extent of being personally befriended by Lord Sandwich, now First Lord of the Admiralty.

Sandwich was an extraordinary person, a notorious rake, an inveterate gambler, and a singularly corrupt official. His personal appearance was so unprepossessing that some wag once described him as looking as if he had been "half-hanged and cut down by mistake." Nevertheless, Sandwich was shrewd enough to realize that by patronizing Cook, he would attract a certain amount of good publicity to himself. From now on he exerted himself to promote Cook's being dispatched on a further voyage of discovery. By way of a start he saw to it that the Admiralty promoted him to the rank of commander.

Not that the Admiralty was unwilling; their Lordships were really delighted. They were just beginning to realize that in the charts of five thousand miles of hitherto unknown coastlines with which Cook had presented them, there was a whole new empire for Britain. Moreover, there was a vast collection of material for botanists and ethnologists to pore over. Cook and those brilliant men who sailed with him had gone to endless trouble describing plants, animals, and people hitherto utterly unknown to the civilized world. It was really no wonder that the king himself summoned Cook to an interview in August.

For the ordinary public, a ponderous account of the whole voyage was being prepared by a certain Dr. John Hawkesworth. It was founded upon the journals of Cook and Banks but it contained some remarkably inaccurate and stupid statements for which neither man was responsible. In preparing the manuscript, Hawkesworth found himself—to use a convenient pun—at sea in more ways than one.

Cook's own journal, greatly preferable to modern readers, was held to be unsuitable owing to its lack of literary embellishment. The erudite world of the eighteenth century believed that for the task of writing any kind of book the services of a professional literary gentleman were indispensable. Thus the actual Journal was not published until 1893.

Cook himself, although he disapproved of Hawkesworth's flowery and ridiculous passages, was aware of his own unsuitability as a writer. In the narrative of his second voyage he was to excuse himself as one "who has been constantly at sea from his youth," and hoped that the reader would "consider me a plain man, zealously exerting himself in the service of his country and determined to give the best account he is able of his proceedings."

In the sunny skies of official commendation and approval and lively public popularity, there was one gloomy depression: that tiresome Scot, Mr. Alexander Dalrymple.

Too obstinate to admit he had made a mistake and jealous of Cook's swift rise to public fame, Dalrymple continued to insist that *Terra Australis* actually existed; if the *Endeavour* hadn't sighted it, that was the fault of the ship herself and her commander. What made matters worse in Dalrymple's opinion was the fact that his own ponderous study of the Pacific had just been published. In it he had made very clear that, as far as he was concerned, the southern continent *did* exist. Cook had now annoyingly proved that it did *not*. Therefore, stated Dalrymple, the continent was actually located in those eastern parts over which the *Endeavour* had not sailed.

Cook himself agreed that a second voyage was essential to settle finally this whole question of a southern continent, "to put an end to all diversity of opinion about a matter so curious and important." The Admiralty fully agreed; the new coastlines, as well as the possibility of others not yet discovered, were as utterly fascinating for them as for British statesmen.

While Dalrymple vented his embittered rage on Hawkesworth's edition of Cook's Journal, suggesting that the commander was a *poseur* and possibly a liar as well, the Admiralty spent its time more profitably in searching for the two vessels that would serve Cook on his second voyage. The old *Endeavour* was no longer in sound condition. She faded into obscurity and ended her days in Newport, Rhode Island, where she gradually rotted to bits.* A replacement for her had to be found, and, as the adventure on the Great Barrier Reef had nearly proved, two ships were infinitely safer than one.

Cook now had some leisure to spend at his home in the Mile End Road. Matters were not satisfactory in that little house. The child Elizabeth Cook had been expecting when the *Endeavour* sailed had died a few days after birth. Three months before the vessel returned, the five-year-old Elizabeth had also died. It was not surprising, of course; children always were dying of some mysterious illness or other in those days. The only surprising thing about that age of abysmal ignorance in hygiene and medicine is that enough of them survived to bring about a natural increase in population.

The Admiralty bought two new Whitby-built vessels originally named *Drake* and *Raleigh*. The *Drake* was one hundred tons larger than the *Endeavour*, the *Raleigh* a little smaller. The names of both ships were changed to *Resolution* and *Adventure*.

The former was to remain Cook's own ship until his death. She was a fine, roomy craft of 460 tons, manned by a crew of 112 and armed with twelve 12-pounder guns. The 336-ton *Adventure* carried a crew of eighty-two and was to be commanded by thirty-seven-year-old Lieutenant Tobias Furneaux, who had sailed with Wallis round the world and already established his reputation as a reliable officer. He came of an ancient family which dated back to the days of the Norman Conquest.

Cook, recently returned from a visit to his sturdy old father now aged seventy-eight and a widower for the past three years, began to assemble his crew in January 1772. Cooper, his first lieutenant, was a friend of Admiral Palliser and an excellent officer.

Lieutenant Gore was also back again, as were Clerke and Pickersgill, both promoted now to commissioned rank and heading for the captaincies they would be awarded in later years. Many of the *Endeavour*'s warrant officers signed on again. So keen was the competition that two young officers, James Burney in the *Adventure*, and fifteen-year-old George Vancouver in the *Resolution*, signed on as able seamen. In later life Burney was to rise to the rank of admiral and become famous as the author of an outstanding history of the Pacific. Captain Vancouver was to find fame as an explorer who became a worthy successor to Captain Cook.

The passengers to accompany the expedition were all new. Banks had reluctantly withdrawn after failing in his excessive demands for lavish and elaborate accommodation aboard the *Resolution*. John Reinhold Forster and his son George were the scientist substitutes who replaced him. They were naturalized Prussians, an obstinate and downright difficult pair, infinitely more interested in themselves and the prospect of enhancing their reputations than they were in the ship or the broader aspects of the forthcoming expedition. An artist called Hodge was included. He was a pleasant fellow, but something of a pompous neoclassicist, a tendency that caused him to depict Polynesians as Greeks or Romans. Wales and Bayley were the two astronomers, whose task it would be to look after the new chronometers which the *Resolution* was to carry.

The successful trial of these newly invented chronometers was to result in the voyage's becoming one of the most important in the history of navigation. Ships would soon be able to establish their longitude without having recourse to the complicated mathematics of lunar calculation or the simpler but less accurate method of tossing a log overboard and timing its drift. (Cook's chronometer, made by a Yorkshireman named John Harrison, is still keeping perfect time at the Royal Observatory in England.)

A modest total of four civilian passengers therefore accompanied the *Resolution*. Bayley the astronomer sailed aboard the *Adventure*.

* Part of her sternpost is now in the local museum at Newport.

Details from the original plans of the *Resolution* (National Maritime Museum).

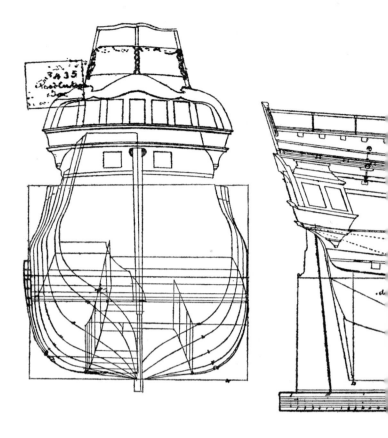

The instructions for the voyage, which Cook himself had helped to draft, ordered him to settle the controversy regarding the southern continent. After passing the Cape of Good Hope, he was to sail east with the Westerlies during the summer and thus attempt to enter higher latitudes than anyone had ever previously attained. The orders particularly stressed that he was to carry out such navigation only during the summer and that in winter he was to withdraw northward into a more favorable climate.

The absence of scurvy during the *Endeavour*'s voyage had encouraged both the Admiralty and Cook himself to increase the anti-scorbutic provisions for the crew of both vessels. In addition to malt and sauerkraut, the rations now included salted cabbage, carrot marmalade, and a curious commodity identified as Inspissated (condensed) Juice of Beer.

Cook sailed from Plymouth on 13 July 1772. He reached Capetown at the end of October. By that time the elder Forster, who was receiving the fantastic sum of £ 4,000 for making the voyage, had made himself thoroughly detested by the entire crew, who rejoiced greatly when he began to complain of severe rheumatic pains.

Cook's first intention was to sight Cape Circumcision far to the south of Africa, which the French explorer Bouvet had reported thirty years previously. The Frenchman had suggested that it might be an outlying point of the southern continent. Bouvet Island actually exists, two thousand miles from the nearest land, but Cook failed to sight it.

"Sunday 3rd January 1773.
We were now about $1\frac{1}{2}°$ or $2°$ of Longitude to the West of the Meridian of Cape Circumcision and at the going down of the sun $4°45'$ of Latitude to the Southward of it, the Weather was so clear that Land even of a Moderate height might have been seen 15 Leagues, so that there could be no Land betwixt us and the Latitude of $48°$. In short I am of the opinion that what Mr. Bouvet took for Land and named Cape Circumcision was nothing but Mountains of Ice surrounded by field Ice."
"Monday 4th January . . .
First and middle parts strong gales attended with a thick Fog, Sleet and Snow, all the Rigging covered with Ice and the air excessive cold, the Crew however stand it tolerably well, each being clothed with a fearnought jacket *[made of wool and thick canvas—RS]*, a pair of Trowsers of the same and a large cap made of Canvas and Baize, these together with an additional glass of Brandy every morning enables them to bear the Cold without flinching."

In mid-January 1773 Cook sailed into the Antarctic Circle (latitude $66° 32'$ south), the first time this feat had ever been accomplished by a navigator. It was an alarming experience for everyone aboard. There were constant gales and heavy seas, the decks and rigging were continuously covered with a dangerous layer of ice. Both icebergs and pack

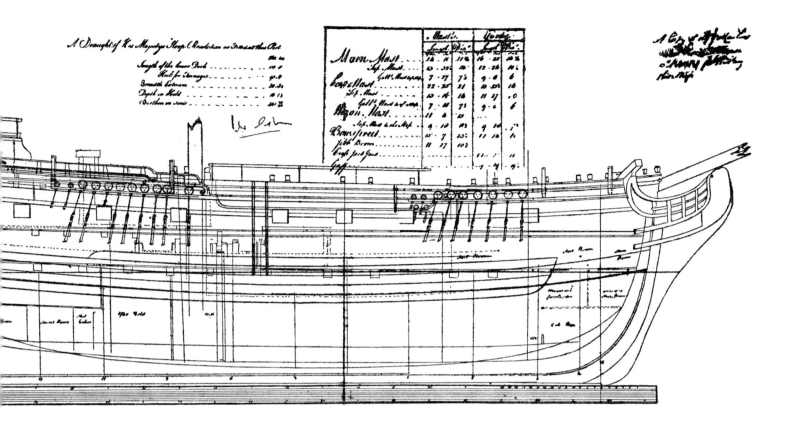

ice continued to make the next two and a half months an ordeal that the Forsters had not in the least expected when they embarked on this voyage to the balmy South Seas.

In February Cook was in the southern Indian Ocean, passing midway between Kerguelen and the Crozet Islands after ice and appalling weather had forced him northward into latitude 50° south. On 9 February the *Resolution* lost sight of the *Adventure* in extremely foggy weather. Signal guns were fired at regular intervals during the afternoon, but when the weather cleared just before darkness there was no sign of Captain Furneaux in his *Adventure*.

Cook was not greatly concerned by this hitch in the voyage. He had already arranged that in the event of the ships' losing contact with each other, they would proceed separately to a rendezvous at Queen Charlotte Sound in New Zealand. Before setting course for the same destination, he made yet another run southward into latitude 67° south,

at which stage it became apparent that no further advance could be attempted.

Cook had carried out a major part of his orders by sailing eastward through 145 degrees of longitude at an average latitude of 60° south. Now he squared away to the east, still in the same latitude for the long run to the meridian of the western coast of Australia. No one could blame him for going to overmuch trouble to prove to the scientific world that Dalrymple's contention was entirely incorrect. The best possible way to prove it was by taking the *Resolution* across the alleged whereabouts of *Terra Australis*.

On 27 March, the *Resolution* under full sail sighted the entrance to Dusky Sound on the extreme southwest coast of New Zealand. For men who had spent 117 days at sea and travelled many thousands of miles out of sight of land, luxuriant pine forests and high green hills proved a welcome sight.

"It may be asked why I did not proceed directly for [Queen Charlotte Sound] as being the Rendezvous. The

Discovery of a good Port in the Southern part of this Country and to find out its produce were objects more interesting, it is quite immaterial whether the *Adventure* joins us now or a Month or two hence. Mention has already been made of sweet wort being given to the Scorbutick People; the Marmalade of Carrots alone was given to one man and we found that both had the desired effect in so much that we have only one man on board that can be called ill of this disease and two or three more on the Sick list of slight complaints."

Two weeks later, the *Resolution* left Dusky Sound and sailed northward along the coast to her rendezvous with the *Adventure* in Queen Charlotte Sound.

Captain Furneaux had already arrived, indeed he had been waiting for the past six weeks and making rather dilatory efforts to cure twenty of his seamen who were badly affected by scurvy. The *Resolution* had only one man sick. Why the difference, Cook demanded?

Furneaux, it seemed, was not altogether convinced that wort, marmalade, and salted cabbage were efficient antiscorbutics. He had neglected to enforce the order that his men eat these special rations regularly. Cook promptly sent one of his own cooks on board the *Adventure* and sharply reminded Furneaux to follow diet instructions more closely in the future.

At the same time he congratulated Furneaux on having planted the parsnips, carrots, and potatoes which King George III, who would certainly have been happier as a farmer than a monarch, had given him for that particular purpose.

"Thursday 3rd June.

Yesterday morning a Man brought his son a boy about 10 years of age and presented him to me and as the report was then current I thought he wanted to sell him, but at last I found out that he wanted me to give him a Shirt which I accordingly did. The boy was so fond of his new dress that he went all over the Ship presenting himself to everybody that came in his way. The liberty of the Boy offended old Will the Ram Goat who up with his head and knock'd the boy backwards on the Deck. Will would have repeated his blow had not some of the people got to the boy's assistance, this misfortune however seem'd to him irrepairable, the Shirt was dirted and he was afraid to appear in the Cabbin before his father, until brought in [by] Mr. Forster, when he told a very lamentable story against Goure the great Dog, for so they call all the quadrupeds we have aboard. [*Kuri*, the Maori word for their own native dogs, which were mute. RS] Nor could he be pacified untill his Shirt was wash'd and dry'd... A trade soon Commenced between our people and these, it was not possible to hinder the former from giving the clothes from their backs for the merest trifles, things that were neither usefull nor curious, such was the prevailing passion for curiosities, and caused me to dismiss these

RESOLUTION

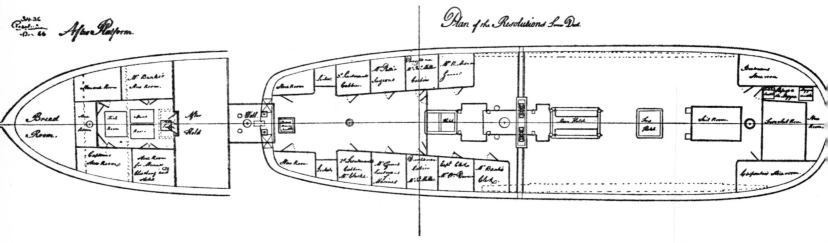

Deck plan of the *Resolution* (National Maritime Museum, Greenwich).

strangers sooner than I would have done. When they departed they went over to Moutara where, by the help of our Glasses we discover'd four or five more Canoes and a number of people on the Shore, this induced me to go over in my boat accompanied by Mr. Forster and one of the Officers. We were well received by the Chief and whole tribe which consisted of between 90 and 100 people, Men, Women and Children, having with them six Canoes and all their utensils, which made it probable that they were come to reside in this Sound, but this is only conjecture for it is very common for them when they even go but a little way to carry their whole property with them, every place being equally alike to them if it affords the necessary subsistance, so that it can hardly be said that they are ever from home, thus we may easily account for the migration of those few small families we found in *Dusky Bay.* Living thus dispersed in small parties, knowing no head but the chief of the family or tribe whose authority may be very little, subjects them to many inconveniences a well regulated society united under one head or any form of government are not subject to, these form Laws and regulations for their general security, are not alarm'd at the appearance of every stranger and if attack'd or invaded by a publick enemy have strong holds to retire to where they can with advantage defend themselves, their property and their country."

As the Antipodean winter was now approaching, Cook decided to spend the next six months exploring in tropical seas.

By the middle of August he was in the latitude of Pitcairn Island, discovered by Captain Carteret in 1767, but in spite of the three-hundred-foot-high peak of this tiny island, which is a mere two square miles in area, he was unable to locate it. Its position had been inaccurately plotted.

Bearing away to the northeast on his course to Tahiti, both ships sighted several of the Paumotu (or Tuamotu) Islands but prudently kept clear of the treacherous reefs, currents, and underwater shoals of those lonely, palm-covered specks of land. In late August, after both ships had nearly come to grief on the underwater coral heads off the coast of Tahiti, anchor was dropped in the familiar, friendly surroundings of Matavai Bay.

But Tahiti, the former paradise of European seamen, was already sadly changed. Hogs and chickens, which formerly had been abundant, were now extremely scarce. Two brief but savage wars had been fought between different tribes, and a

Watercolor detail of the *Resolution* by John Webber, made during Cook's third voyage (British Museum).

CAPTIONS OF PLATES 47–55

47 "*They also had wood carved human figures; although the features of these were not pleasant, the whole carving shows a certain sense of arts. These figures seemed to be very precious to them.*"
Carved wooden ancestor figure from Easter Island.

48 "*I can not tell anything about their amusements for we never met them doing something like this; but at least they seemed to be very fond of dancing, for they often talked about it.*"
Janus-faced dance paddle from Easter Island. The carving is almost exactly the same on both sides (Museum für Völkerkunde, Vienna).

49, 51, 52 "*These natives all dispose of an admirable artistic skill; there seemed to be nothing they could not represent in their carving.*"
(49) Carved wooden figure of a Haida medicine man. On the back of the figure there is a label of the Missionary Leaves Association with the following inscription: "*Hydah Medicine Man. This man was lost in the woods. He fell and broke both legs, and was found as represented here – starved to death*" (British Museum).
(51) Eagle totem pole from Alert Bay, Vancouver Island; Kwakiutl. Now at the University of British Columbia, Vancouver.
(52) Detail from the totem pole of Chief Git-dum-kuldoah in Gitanmaks, British Columbia.

50 "*The land appeared to be of a moderate height, and, almost every where, covered with wood.*"
Early morning at Queen Charlotte Islands, British Columbia, center of the Haida region.

53 "*They confess that they owe to the bears all their skill both in physic and surgery; they acknowledge them likewise for their dancing masters.*"
Cloak, woven from vegetable fibers and goat hair, used by the Chilkats, one of the Tlingit tribes, for ceremonies and dances. The design represents a bear. British Columbia.

54, 55 "*From the elevated spot on which Mr. King surveyed the surrounding, he could distinguish an extensive valley of a river.*"
(54) Night at the Skeena River, British Columbia.
(55) Rock painting of the Kitksan Indians in the valley of the Skeena River.

47

48

49

50

51

52

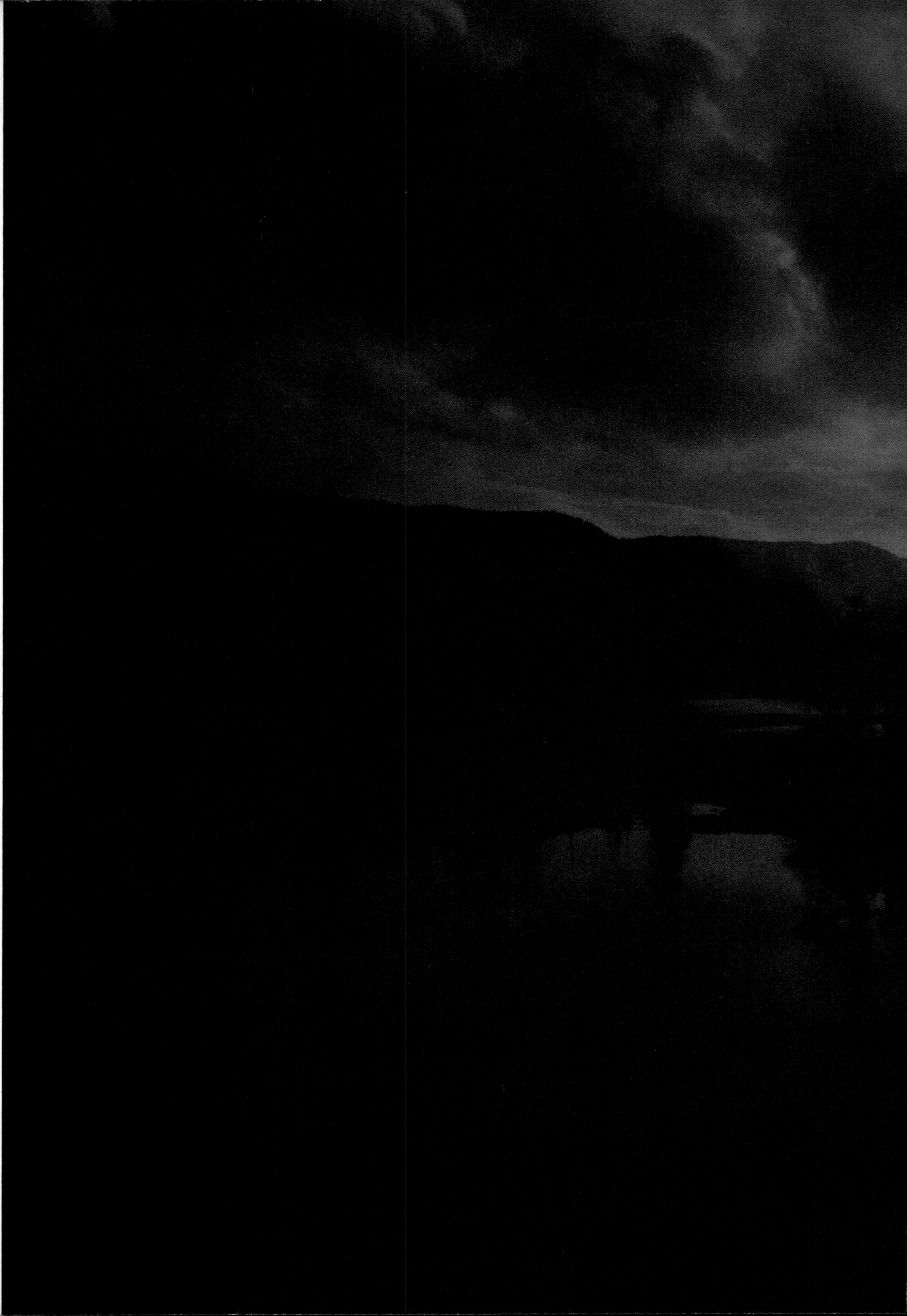

number of the population had died during an epidemic of a previously unknown sickness that may have been gastric influenza. The former gaiety and carefree spirit of the island was swiftly diminishing. Somehow the people appeared to sense that never again would their island be the same. The white strangers, although they were friendly and gave gifts while everlastingly pursuing the young women, were simultaneously destroying the traditional way of life. The pattern of the white man's activities in the South Pacific was already being shaped.

Leaving Tahiti at the beginning of September, Cook sailed westward to other islands in the Society Group, including the adjacent island of Moorea, a mere eleven miles from Tahiti, and to the more distant, high, and fertile island of Huahine. With Cook went a young, dark-skinned Tahitian named Omai, the only Polynesian who was to be successful in visiting Europe and in returning alive to his own land. (Otiti, another young man who also sailed, did not survive Europe.)

"Sunday 5th September.

[At Huahine] Early in the morning Oree made me a visit accompanied by some of his friends. He brought me a present of a Hog and some fruit for which I made him a suitable return, this good old Chief never fail'd to send me every day for my Table the best of ready dress'd fruit and roots and in great plenty. Lieut. Pickersgill was again detached to the South end of the Island with both Cutter and Launch, he returned the same day with Twenty-eight hogs and about four times as many more were got ashore and alongside the Sloops."

The westward voyage across the Pacific continued. Cook was anxious to find further islands, including the Friendly or Tonga group, containing the islands named Amsterdam and Middelburg discovered by Tasman in 1643 but not since revisited—fortunately for them—by any European vessel. After sighting one or two of the smaller and hitherto unknown islands of the southern Cook Group, the ships reached Tongatabu on 2 October.

"At 8 o'Clock we discovered a small Island lying WSW from the South end of Middleburg, not knowing but these two Islands might be connected to each other by a reef the extent of which we might be ignorant of and in order to guard against the worst, we haul'd the wind and spent the night making short boards under an easy sail ... Soon after we had come to an Anchor, I went a Shore with Captain Furneaux and some of the Officers and gentlemen, having in the Boat with us Tioonee who conducted us to the proper landing place where we were welcomed a shore by acclamations from an immense crowd of Men and Women not one of which had so much as a stick in their hands, they crowded so thick round the boats with Cloth, Matting, &ca. to exchange for Nails that it was some time before we could get room to land, at last the Chief cleared the way and conducted us up to his house which was situated hard by in a most delightfull spot, the floor was laid with Matting on which we were seated, the Islanders who accompanied us seated themselves in a circle round the out sides. I ordered the Bagpipes to be pla[y]ed and in return the Chief ordered three young women to Sing a Song which they did with a very good grace. When they had done I gave each a necklace, this set most of the Women in the Circle a Singing, their songs were musical and harmonious, no ways harsh or disagreeable ... Captain Furneaux and I were conducted to the Chiefs house where we had fruit brought us to eat, afterwards he accompanied us into the Country through several Plantations Planted with Fruit trees, roots &ca in great taste and ellegancy and enclosed by neat fences made of reeds. In the lanes and about their house were running about Hogs and large fowls which were the only domestic Animals we saw and these they did not seem desireous to part with, nor did they during this day offer to exchange any fruit or roots worth mentioning, this determined me to leave the Island [Eua] in the morning and go down to that of Amsterdam where Tasman in 1643 found refreshments in plenty. In the evening we all returned aboard, every one highly dilighted with his little excursion and the friendly behaver of the Natives, who seem'd to [vie] with each other in doing what they thought would give us pleasure."

During the ships' stay in the Tonga Group, Cook was quick to notice significant differences between the Tahitians and the Tongans. The latter were more serious, better-disciplined, and although their desire for iron articles was extremely keen, they seldom if ever resorted to cunning trickery to obtain it. In short, they appeared to be of higher and more worthwhile character altogether. It was patent that the younger women, even those of the lower classes, were much less indiscriminate in the favors they granted the ardent sailors. The Tongans were also more strongly built and a great deal more industrious than the Tahitians; a difference which is still noticeable two hundred years later. Their growing dislike of the worthless and rapacious types of Europeans who visited their islands over the years was to give them a justifiable reputation as "a nation of wreckers." It was a reputation that fortunately helped to preserve them from degradation at the hands of the sandalwood traders and slavers.

"Monday 4th October.

After breakfast I went ashore with Captain Furneaux, Mr. Forster and several of the officers. A chief or man of some note to whom I had made several presents was in the Boat with us. His name was Hātago, by which name he desired I might be called and he by mine [Otootee]. We were lucky in having anchored before a narrow creek in the rocks which just admitted our Boats within the breakers where they laid secure and at high water we could land dry on the shore; into this place Hātago conducted us; there on the shore an immense crowd of men, Women and children who welcomed us in the same manner as those of Middleburg and were like them all unarm'd. All the officers and gentlemen set out into the Country as soon as we landed, excepting Captain Furneaux who stayed with me on the shore, we two Hātago seated on the grass and ordered the People to set down in a circle round us which they did, never once attempting to push themselves upon us as the Otahieteans and the people of the neighbouring Isles generally do. After distributing some trifles among them we signified our desire to see the Country. This was no sooner done than the chief shewed us the way, conducting us along a lane which led us to an open green on the one side of which was a house of Worship built on a Mount which had been raised by the hand of Man about 16 or 18 feet above the common level . . . After we had done examining this place of worship which, in their Language is called *Afiā-tou-ca,* we desired to return, but instead of conducting us directly to the Waterside, they struck into a road leading into the Country. This road, which was a very public one, was about 15 feet broad and as even as a Bowling green. There was a fence of reeds on each side and here and there doors which opened into the adjoining Plantations. Several other Roads from different parts joined this, some equally broad and others narrower, the most part of them shaded from the Scorching Sun by fruit trees. I thought I was transported into one of the most fertile plains in Europe, here was not an inch of waste ground, the road occupied no more space than was absolutely necessarey, and each fence did not take up above 4 inches, and even this was not wholly lost, for in many of the fences were planted fruit trees and the Cloth plant, these served as a support to them. It was everywhere the same, change of place altered not the scene. Nature, assisted by a little art, nowhere appears in a more florishing state than at this Isle. In these delightfull walks we met numbers of people, some were travelling down to the Ships with their burdens of fruit, others returning back empty, they all gave us the road and either sat down or stood up with their backs against the fences till we had passed . . . As soon as diner was over we all went ashore again where we found the old Chief who presented me with a Hog and he and some others took a walk with us into the Isle, our rout[e] was by the first-mentioned *Afiā-tou-ca* before which we again seated ourselves, but had no praying; on the contrary here the good natured old Chief interduced to me a woman and gave me to understand that I might retire with her, she was next offered to Captain Furneaux but met with a refusal from both, tho she was neither old nor ugly, our stay here was but short. The Chief probably thinking that we might want water on board the Sloops conducted us to a Plantation hard by and there shewed us a pool of fresh Water without our making the least enquiry after such a thing. I believe it to be the same as Tasman calls the Washing place for the King and his nobles."

The southern summer was now imminent and with it came the cheerless prospect of another voyage to the Antarctic. It was with the most profound regret that the captains and crew of both vessels bade farewell to Nukualofa and the smaller but almost equally attractive island of Eua in the Tonga Group, to which Cook had now given the name of the Friendly Islands.

A major setback which marred the voyage occurred as the two ships were approaching the entrance to Cook Strait. A gale blew up and the *Adventure* was lost to sight. By excellent seamanship Cook brought the *Resolution* into Queen Charlotte Sound. The *Adventure* did not reappear during the next three weeks, for she had been driven much farther to the eastward and had to tack endlessly in order to regain the Sound. As it was now November, Cook could wait no longer for fear of losing much of the summer season. He left the Sound on 25 November, after leaving sealed instructions for Furneaux buried in a bottle beside the stump of a tree.

The *Adventure* arrived four days later, but the parting was final. Henceforward the voyage became that of two separate vessels.

FROM THE ANTARCTIC TO MELANESIA

ook sailed the *Resolution* first southward and then southeastward from New Zealand to approximately 60° south latitude and then twice crossed the Antarctic Circle in the longitude of Tahiti. On 30 January 1774 he reached latitude 71° 10′ south, where, in approximately the same longitude as Mexico City, he was barred any further progress by an immense barrier of ice.

He was now more than four degrees within the Antarctic Circle, and as one modern geographer has said: "no one again reached this latitude for half a century, and no one has reached it in that area since Cook."

In February the vessel was still south of the Antarctic circle. "The whole scene," wrote the elder Forster, "looked like the wreck of a shattered world, or as the poets describe some regions of hell; an idea which struck us the more forcibly as execrations, oaths and curses re-echoed about us on all sides."

It was now up to Cook whether he returned home or carried on exploring in the Pacific for another summer. His crew was in excellent health, the vessel sound, and victuals still remained in abundance. He had entirely satisfied himself that no continent existed in these far southern waters, and he was of the opinion that the summer could be much better spent exploring the tropics.

"Sunday 6th February [1774].

In the AM we got the wind from the South, loosed all the reefs out, got top-gt yards and set the sails and steered North-Easterly, with a resolution to proceed directly to the North as there was no probability of finding Land in these high Latitudes, at least not on this side Cape Horn and I thought it equally as improbable any should be found on the other side. But supposing the Land laid down in Mr. Dalrymple's Chart to exist, or that of Bouvet, before we could reach the one or the other the Season would be too far spent to explore it this Summer, and obliged us either to have wintered upon it, or retired to Falkland Isles or the Cape of Good Hope. Whichever had been done, Six or Seven Months must have been spent without being able in that time to make any discovery whatever, but if we had met with no land or impediment we might have reached the last of these places by April at farthest, when the expedition would have been finished so far as it related to the finding of a Southern Continent, mentioned by all Authors who have written on this subject, whose assertions and conjectures are now entirely refuted as all their enquiries were confined to this Southern Pacific Ocean in which, altho' there lies no continent there is however room for very large islands. And many of those formerly discover'd within the Southern Tropick are very imperfectly explored and their situation as imperfectly known. All these things considered, and more especially as I had a good Ship, a healthy crew and no want of stores or Provisions I thought I cou'd not do better than to spend the ensuing Winter within the Tropicks. I must own I have little expectation of making any valuable discovery, nevertheless it must be allowed that the Sciences will receive some improvement therefrom especially Navigation and Geography. I had several times communicated my thoughts on this subject to Captain Furneaux, at first he seem'd not to approve of it, but was inclinable to get to the Cape of Good Hope. Afterwards he seem'd to come to my opinion; I however could not well give any Instructions about it, as that time it depended on so many circumstances and therefore cannot even guess how Captain Furneaux will act. Be this as it will, my intention is now to go in search of the Land said to be discovered by Juan Fernandes in the Latitude of 38°, not finding any such Land, to look for Easter Island, the situation of which is so variously laid down that I have little hopes of finding. I next intend to get within the Tropicks and proceed to the west on a route differing from former Navigators, touching at, and settling the Situation of such Isles as we may meet with, and if I have time, to proceed in this manner as far west as Quiros's Land, or what M. de Bougainville calls the Great Cyclades. Quiros describes this Land, which he calls Tierra Austral del Espiritu Santo, as being very large."

On 11 March 1774 the *Resolution* sighted Easter Island, discovered by the Dutch navigator Roggeveen on Easter Sunday 1722.

This thirteen-mile-long island lies 2030 miles from the coast of South America, and at that time was inhabited by an unusual variety of the Polynesian race. It was, in fact, the most easterly island settled by the Polynesian navigators during their centuries-long migration across the ocean from the coast of Indo-China. Easter Island was to become famous in modern times for possessing the only stone houses ever built by the Polynesians and for the great stone heads carved by the vanished people. The origin of those stone heads as well as the mysterious fate of the inhabitants are still among the world's most famous archaeological puzzles.

The population was decimated in 1862 by Peruvian slavers, and, in typical manner, the early missionaries lacked the vision and culture to collect history and legends from the demoralized survivors.

"Tuesday 15th March.

Got on board a few Casks of Water and Traded with the Natives for some of the produce of the island which appeared in no great plenty and the Water so bad as not to be worth carrying on board, and the ship not in safety determined me to shorten my stay here."

From Easter Island the *Resolution* sailed northeast through the Tuamotu Islands and on 7 April came to the mountainous and lovely Marquesas.

Cook was the first seaman to reach this group of islands since Mendaña had discovered them in 1595. The population, which in those days may possibly have numbered one hundred thousand Polynesians, termed themselves the Tăkĕ (Cause of Life). Many of their customs and legends differed from those found elsewhere in Polynesia; in physique and appearance they were the most handsome and intelligent race that Cook had yet encountered; a race worthy of their own magnificent islands.

"Tuesday 12th April.

These Isles as I have before observed were first discovered by Mendena and by him called Marquesas, he likewise gave names to the different isles. The Nautical description of them in Mr. Dalrymple's Collection of Voyages is deficient in nothing but Situation, and this was the chief point I wanted to settle and my reason for touching at them, as it will in a great measure fix the Situation of all Mendena's discoveries ... The Inhabitants of these Isles are without exceptions as fine a race of people as any in this Sea or perhaps any whatever; The Men are Tattowed or curiously Marked from head to foot which makes then look dark but the Women (who are but little Tattow'd) youths and young children are as fair as some Europeans, they clothe themselves with the Same sort of Cloth and Matting as the Otaheiteans; they wear as Ornaments a kind of Fillit curiously ornamented with Tortoise and Mother of Pearl Shells, Feathers &ca. Round their necks an ornament of this form, it is made with Wood on which are stuck with gum a great number of small red Pease, they also wear bunches of human hair round their legs and arms &ca.

The men in general are tall that is about six feet high, but we saw none so lusty as at Otaheite and the neighbouring isles, nevertheless they are of the same race of People, their language, customs &ca all tend to prove it.

They dwell in the Vallies and on the sides of the hills near their plantations, their Houses are built after the same manner as at Otaheite, but are much meaner and only covered with the leaves of the bread tree. They have also dwellings or Strong holds on the summits of the highest Mountains, these we saw by the help of our Glasses for I did not permit any of our people to go to them [for] fear of being attack'd by the Natives whose dispositions we were not sufficiently acquainted with."

Much to the regret of his crew, who desired to prolong their stay in this unspoiled Eden and attempt furtive conquests of the handsome and independent Marquesan women, Cook was anxious to return to Tahiti. The *Resolution* again dropped anchor in Matavai Bay on 22 April.

For some obscure reason—and logical reasons can still be difficult to obtain anywhere in Polynesia—the Tahitian people had decided to go to war with the population of the neighboring island of Moorea, which the people then called Eimeo. The men of the *Resolution* had a unique opportunity to see the Tahitian war-fleet being prepared. It was a spectacle never seen again by European eyes.

"When we had got into our boat we took our time to view this fleet, the Vessels of War consisted of 160 large double Canoes, very well equip'd, Man'd and Arm'd, altho' I am not sure that they had on board either their full complement of Fighting men or rowers, I rather think not. The Chief and all those on the Fighting Stages were dressed in their War habits, that is in a vast quantity of Cloth, Turbands, breast Plates and Helmets, some of the latter are of such a length as to greatly incumber the wearer, indeed their whole dress seem'd ill calculated for the day of Battle and seems to be design'd more for Shew than use. Be this as it may they certainly added grandeur to the Prospect, as they were complacent enough to Shew themselves to the best advantage, their Vessels were decorated with Flags, Streamers &ca so that the whole made a grand and Noble appearance such as was never seen before in this Sea. Their implements of war were Clubs, pikes and Stones. These Canoes were ranged close alongside each other with their heads ashore and Sterns to the Sea, the Admirals vessel was, as near as I could guess, in the center. Besides these vessels of War there were 170 Sail of Smaller double Canoes all with a little house upon them and rigg'd with Masts and sails which the others had not; These Canoes must be design'd for transport or Victuallers or both, and to receive the wounded Men &ca. In the War Canoes were no sort of Provisions whatever. In these 303 Canoes I judged there were no less than 7760 Men, a number which appears incredible, especially as we were told that they all belonged to the districts of Attahourou and Ahopatea; in this computation I allow to each War Canoe, one with another, 40 Men, rowers and fighting Men, and to each of the Small Canoes eight, but most of the gentlemen who saw this fleet thinks the number of Men to the War Canoes were more than I have reckoned...."

The steady southeast trade winds of the crisp and vigorous Pacific winter encouraged Cook to renew his exploration of the western Pacific. As their vessel headed away from the palm-shaded beaches lined with brown-skinned Tahitians waving farewell, the seamen of the *Resolution* moodily brooded that none of them might ever come this way again. The thought was too much for an Irish gunner's mate, James Marra, who slid overboard and began to swim to the shore. He was a silent, lonely fellow who seemed without a friend in the world. A boat was sent after him and he was brought back on board. Cook, with typical humanity, made the comment that if only the sailor had asked for permission to remain in Tahiti he would probably have received it, but now the poor fellow had lost his chance forever.

Cook called at Niue Island, halfway between the undiscovered island of Rarotonga and Tonga, and promptly named it Savage Island because a local warrior threw an ill-aimed spear at him. (This fact was resented by later generations of Niueans. They had no desire to be remembered merely as bad marksmen.)

Fernandes de Quiros, a Portuguese pilot who sailed with a fellow-Portuguese explorer, Luis Vaez de Torres, in 1605, had mistakenly believed that the New Hebrides were part of a great southern continent, which he named Australia del Espiritu Santo. Cook was determined to make a more thorough investigation of this territory.

The New Hebrides, as Cook named them, were dark, damp, and covered with gloomy forest. They came as a great disappointment to him. He sailed down their eastern coasts, and then northward up the western coasts until he reached the vast bay of Espiritu Santo. Nowhere did he find the people attractive. They were thin, bushy-haired, Negroid in appearance and many were suffering from skin diseases including yaws. They formed a strong contrast with the handsome, lightskinned Polynesians of the eastern Pacific, their customs and way of life being both dissimilar and inferior.

There is no doubt that the New Hebrideans were plotting mischief against the *Resolution*'s crew, but their primitive minds and lack of disciplined organization made it difficult for them to know how best to proceed.

"I landed [from one of the ship's boats] in the face of a great Multitude with nothing but a green branch in my hand I had got from one of them. I was received very courteously and upon my makeing Signs to keep off, one Man who seem'd to be a Chief amongst them at once comprehending what I meant, made them form a kind of Semicircle round the bow of the boat and beat any one who broke through this order.... I was charmed with their behaviour, the only thing which could give the least Suspicion was the most of them being Arm'd with Clubs, Darts, stones and bows and Arrows. The Chief made a sign to me to haul the Boat up upon the Shore, but I gave him to understand that I must first go on board and then I would return and do what he desired and so step'd into the boat and ordered her to be put off. But they were not for parting with us so soon and now attempted by force to accomplish what they could not obtain by more gentler means. The gang-board having been put out for me to come in, some seized hold of it while others snatched hold of the Oars. Upon my pointing a musket at them, they in some measure desisted, but return'd again in an instant, seemingly ditermined to haul the boat up upon Shore. At the head of this party was the Chief, and the others who had not room to come at the boat stood ready with their darts and bows and arrows to support them: our own safety became now the only consideration and yet I was very loath to fire upon such a Multitude and resolved to make the chief alone fall a Victim to his own treachery, but my musket at this critical Moment refused to perform its part and made it absolutely necessary for me to give orders to fire, as they now began to Shoot their Arrows and throw darts and Stones at us. The first discharge threw them into confusion but another discharge was hardly sufficient to drive them off the beach and after all they continued to throw Stones from behind the trees and bushes, and one would peep out now and then and throw a dart, four laid to all appearance dead on the shore, but two of them afterwards cript into the bushes, happily for many of these people not half our Muskets would go off otherwise many more must have fallen . . . ."*

On his way south to New Zealand at the end of August, Cook sighted a large and mountainous island which he named New Caledonia. This was an important and entirely new discovery, but with the approach of the Antarctic season, Cook was able to spend only ten days examining some of its coast. The Melanesian inhabitants were of a much higher type than those of the New Hebrides and were the only Pacific natives who did not indulge an enormous propensity for theft. They had, however, some strange ideas.

One man offered Cook a large and rather ugly fish as a present. He shared it with the Forsters, and later that evening all three men were seized with a violent fever, giddiness, and loss of all sensation. They dosed themselves with a strong emetic and thereby probably saved their lives, for the gourd fish, or *ue* of Eastern Melanesia, while excellent to eat, contains an extremely poisonous sac which must be removed before the fish is cooked. When the natives came aboard the following morning and heard what had occurred, they casually mentioned that everyone knew that the *ue* was a poisonous fish. Yet none of them had mentioned this fact to Cook when they saw him take the fish the previous evening; a casual attitude often found, it must be admitted, amongst most of the people of the South Pacific.

Five weeks later, the *Resolution* dropped anchor again in Queen Charlotte Sound. They found that the buried message they had left for Captain Furneaux had been removed but no enlightening information left in its place. Nor were the local Maori at all anxious to discuss Furneaux and the

Adventure, most of them appearing extremely ill at ease when Cook brought the subject up.

(It turned out later that Furneaux had reached the Sound four days after Cook sailed for Antarctic waters. While the *Adventure* lay at anchor, a boat's crew of one midshipman and ten sailors had been killed and eaten by the Maori as the result of some sudden quarrel. Furneaux had left New Zealand at the end of 1773 and sailed eastward in high latitudes between 56° and 61° south. After passing several hundred miles south of Cape Horn, he crossed the South Atlantic, called in at Capetown, and thence returned to England, whither he arrived in July 1774. He thus became the first sea captain to circumnavigate the globe in an easterly direction.)

As an explorer, Furneaux like Wallis was handicapped by his naval training. He was accustomed to obey orders and refrain from thinking for himself. He put the safety of his ship and crew first, did as he was told, and seldom showed unusual initiative. He died in 1781.

On 10 November 1774 the *Resolution* headed out to sea on her long voyage back to England via Cape Horn.

During the first part of the homeward trip Cook steered through latitudes 51° to 55° south, but after sighting no land on the way altered course on 27 November and made direct for Cape Horn.

"I have now done with the Southern Pacific Ocean. I hope those who honoured me and flatter myself that no one will think that I have left it unexplored or that more could have been done in one voyage towards obtaining that end than has been done in this."

On his way across the South Atlantic to Capetown, Cook remained in a high latitude and was ill-rewarded with a single discovery: that of the bleak islands of New Georgia and Sandwich Land. He reached South Africa a month later.

On 29 July 1775, more than three years after his departure, he arrived at Plymouth. Of the 112 men who had sailed in the *Resolution*, three men had suffered accidental deaths and a fourth had died from some unknown disease that was certainly not scurvy.

---

* The average musket of those days misfired once in every 10 shots and undoubtedly more frequently in the humidity of the New Hebrides.

56 *"The rising grounds were entirely covered with tall, straight trees. The whole had now an uncomfortable appearance; as the bare mountains were all covered with snow."*
Mountain range at Skeena River, British Columbia. About these mountains are woven countless legends of the Tsimshian, Haida, and Kitksan Indians.

57, 58, 68 *"Their carved wooden masks are of the greatest variety."*
Kitksan masks from the Treasure House of Gitanmaks, British Columbia.
(57) A mask of the Crooked Face secret society.
(58) Mask probably representing the moon.
(68) Headpiece of a chief of the Frog Clan.

59, 62, 67 *"We found the village, the high carved posts were to see from a far distance."*
(59) Reconstruction of a Haida Longhouse, University of British Columbia, Vancouver.
(62) Evening at Gitanmaks, British Columbia, a reconstructed Indian village.
(67) The totem poles of Kitwanga at night. British Columbia.

60, 63, 66 *"The house which I examined, was decorated with monstrous carved posts and showed a floor sunk a little below the surface of the earth."*
Chief Kow-ish-te's community house, Shakes Island, Stkine harbor. The original carvings and house posts of this reconstructed Tlingit house are from the middle of the 18th century.

61 *"They have large, broad or spreading faces; which, upon the whole, were flat. Their eyes, though not small, scarcely bore a proportion to the size of their faces; and their noses had full, round points."*
The face of a Kitksan Indian from Gitanmaks, British Columbia.

64, 65 *"What their notions are of the Deity, and of a future state, I know not. Nothing having been seen that could give us an insight into it."*

(64) Mask representing a strangled man. The Indians believe that this mask and the small dolls found with it were used to cast spells. From the grave of a Shaman (see plate 65).
(65) A Shaman's grave. In 1970 the wind blew over a burnt-out cedar tree, and four cedar boxes which were hidden in the tree fell out. According to local Indians, it was the burial place of an important Shaman with all the paraphernalia of his calling. Tlingit. West coast of Prince of Wales Island, Alaska (Both 64 and 65 are the property of Mr. Terry R. Wills, Alaska).

69 *"The person who played the orator held, in each hand, something which rattled as he kept shaking it."*
Wooden rattle of the Nootka tribes (Klejman collection, New York).

70 *"And there is an island lying before the other."*
Baranof and Chichagof Islands, Alaska.

71 *"The sides were made of one piece, bent round and carved."*
Carved box of cedar wood, found at a Tlingit cremation site 75 miles north of Ketchikon, Alaska (Property of Mr. John Grainger, Alaska).

72, 73 *"It was not possible to get one of their bone carvings, some of which were highly expressive."*
Two ivory carvings, Eskimo, Alaska (Klejman collection, New York). The mother and child shown on plate 72 probably illustrate part of the legend of the Bear Clan, which originated with the marriage of an Indian woman to the chief of the bears. The resulting child was partly human, partly bear, and the sharp teeth inherited from the father's side caused awful pain to the nursing mother.

74 *"The trees, in general, grow with great vigour, and are all of a large size."*
Forest near the Indian village Gitanmaks, British Columbia.

57

58

59

60

61

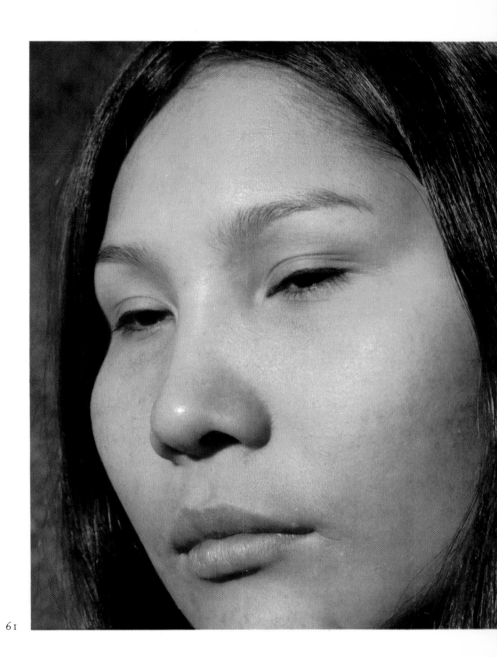

63

64

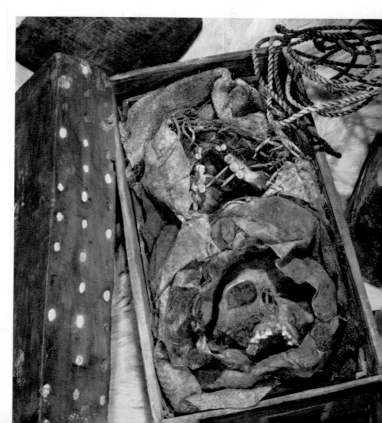

65

67

68

69
70

71

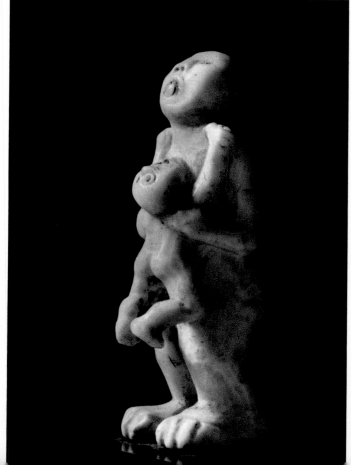

72

THE THIRD VOYAGE

he results of Cook's second voyage convinced him that although an Antarctic Continent might exist it was a relatively small one and of no interest—at least in those days—to the civilized world. So much for Mr. Dalrymple. In the Pacific Cook had made two tremendous sweeps during which he discovered totally unknown islands including New Caledonia and Niue Island, and rediscovered the Tongas, Easter Island, the Marquesas, and the New Hebrides. He had thus created an accurate map of the South Pacific which left little for his successors to do.

His great service to mankind was a demonstration that the careful inclusion of anti-scorbutics in the diet of a ship's crew resulted in almost complete immunity to scurvy.* This discovery was to affect even the design of later naval and merchant ships. Instead of carrying enormous crews to counteract a shortage through scurvy casualties during a long voyage, accommodation could henceforth be more limited and crews considerably smaller.

When Cook had returned home from the first voyage four years earlier, no one outside the Navy had heard of him. Now, at the age of forty-seven years, he was famous throughout the country.

Lord Sandwich, whose administration of the Navy had not enhanced his already unpleasant reputation, again used Cook's latest achievement to attract favorable comment to himself. But he also saw to it that promotion to the rank of captain was given Cook, who only five years earlier had been merely an obscure lieutenant.

More favors followed each other: another interview with the king; promotion to a position that was practically a sinecure at Greenwich Hospital, a home for pensioned seamen; election as a Fellow of the Royal Society in token of his successful

campaign against scurvy; and the recognition and high approval of the scientific world for having proved the worth of Harrison's chronometer as an instrument by means of which longitude could be easily and accurately determined.

Probably it was the position at Greenwich Hospital which interested Cook the most. During his absence, Elizabeth and the two boys Nathaniel and James, now aged ten and eleven, had been financially supported by the charity of Lord Sandwich. Apart from the arrears of pay due him, Cook had no financial resources of his own. England was full of Navy captains for whom no ships were available, and it had seemed to Cook that he might shortly be joining their numbers. But the Greenwich Hospital appointment paid £ 200 a year, and a suite of rooms went with it, not to mention certain small but useful daily allowances. He himself was not over-enthusiastic about the appointment, but at least it meant security for his wife and children, whose future he often worried about.

To John Walker of Whitby, his old employer, Cook wrote:

"I must tell you the *Resolution* was found to answer on all occasions even beyond my expectations, and is so little injured by the voyage that she will soon be sent out again. But I shall not command her. My fate drives me from one extreme to another; a few months ago the whole southern hemisphere was hardly big enough for me, and now I am going to be confined within the limits of Greenwich Hospital, which are far too small for an active mind like mine. I must confess, however, it is a fine retreat and a pretty income, but whether I can bring myself to like ease and retirement, time will show . . ."

Whatever spare time Cook had after his return was devoted to preparing for publication an account of the second voyage. Although the tiresome Forsters aggressively demanded leave to undertake the work, Cook managed to persuade the Admiralty that the pair should not be entrusted with the task. The commission was handed to Canon Douglas, who ultimately produced an infinitely more accurate and distinguished manuscript than the terrible hash created by John Hawkesworth, the ex-schoolmaster.

* Although he failed to give proper appreciation to citrus, the most valuable anti-scorbutic.

Wooden writing tablet from Easter Island. Of all Oceanic peoples, only the aborigines of Easter Island had a form of writing, which still remains undeciphered.

Cook's exploration of the Pacific revived an old and favorite topic of conversation at erudite dining tables. Cargoes from Asia were increasing in volume and frequency, especially the highly valuable ones of silk and tea. At that time such cargoes were being brought to England via the Cape of Good Hope, an extremely long, arduous, and costly voyage. For two hundred years there had been much speculation as to the possible existence of a Northwest Passage between the Atlantic and the Pacific, for such a route would be infinitely shorter and also a great deal safer in time of war. A Scottish fur-trader named Samuel Hearne had approached the problem from the east, by going overland into the Arctic Circle to the northwest of Hudson Bay, without finding any trace of the Passage. Vitus Bering, the Danish explorer, had already given his name in 1728 to the strait which runs between Alaska and Asia, but details of his discovery were not well known by the Admiralty. Was Asia divided from America by this legendary Passage? Was America joined to the frozen lands already explored by Bering? Was there a fair chance of being able to discover the western entrance to an elusive but much-coveted Northwest Passage?

The Admiralty reached a decision: Lieutenant Pickersgill would be sent on a voyage of exploration to the extreme northeast coasts of the Pacific Ocean. No one could decently ask Cook to undertake yet another voyage when surely he was entitled to some rest and leisure ashore.

It was Cook himself who changed that viewpoint. Perhaps by February 1776 he had come to the conclusion that he could not endure being "confined within the limits of Greenwich Hospital." Perhaps, like most of his crew, he found Europe squalid and depressing after the bright skies and unravaged beauty of the Pacific islands. Formal, stuffy contacts with fellow Europeans were infinitely less inspiring than the uninhibited affection and thoughtless generosity of the brown-skinned people of Polynesia.

Cook abruptly volunteered to lead the expedition. The Admiralty hurriedly and gratefully accepted his offer.

The *Resolution* was to sail again, but this time she would be accompanied by another Whitby collier, the *Discovery*, of less than three hundred tons. The latter vessel was to be commanded by Charles Clerke, whose commission Cook arranged after the completion of the first voyage. Through no fault of his own, this unfortunate man had fallen into debt after his return from the sea, and had been forced to take refuge from his debtors in a filthy London slum. While existing in this state of utter poverty, he developed the consumption that was soon to destroy him.

As first lieutenant to Clerke was James Burney, the midshipman of the previous voyage, now commissioned and heading fast for fame. George Vancouver, eighteen years old and also destined for fame, was to serve as a midshipman aboard the *Discovery*.

Serving as lieutenants in the *Resolution* under Cook were John Gore, the veteran of the Pacific, James King, and John Williamson—the one officer doomed to become a failure. The master was William Bligh, who would later gain worldwide recognition from *Mutiny on the Bounty*, figuring for the first time as a turbulent, violent, and competent but quarrelsome man. Bayley the astronomer was to sail again, but a Swiss artist named Webber replaced the classical-minded Hodge. Omai the Tahitian, after more than three years of a delightfully spoiled and pampered existence in London as the darling of society, was to be returned aboard the *Resolution* to his home island of Huahine. By this time Omai had been completely ruined by civilization and rendered entirely unfit to resume a less complicated existence amongst his own people.

The purpose of the third voyage was to attempt to discover a navigable and commercial sea passage from the Pacific to the Atlantic, or, in the Admiralty's own words: "Search for and explore such rivers or inlets as may appear to be of considerable extent, and pointing towards Hudson's or Baffin's Bays."

Almost as an afterthought, the Admiralty added that if no such passage existed, Cook might proceed to look for a Northeast Passage round northern Russia to European seas.

King George, his interest in agriculture undiminished by the imminent revolution of the American colonies, insisted on carrying so much livestock in the shape of horses, goats, sheep, and a number of pigs that Cook, in a letter to Lord Sandwich, described the *Resolution*—now an aging and unsound ship—as "A Noah's Ark, lacking only a few females of our own species."

The interesting comment has been made elsewhere that these British explorers of the eighteenth century attempted to aid rather than exploit the simple peoples of the South Seas. They were the only ones who ever did.

The *Resolution* sailed on 12 July 1776, but the *Discovery* did not leave England until 1 August. After repairs to the seams of both ships at Capetown, they sailed in company to Tasmania, which Cook still believed to be a southerly point of the Australian continent.

They reached this destination on 24 January 1777 and, while collecting firewood in quantities and also grass for the livestock, became friendly with the local natives, a much more attractive and modest people, declared Cook, than the inhabitants of the more northerly parts of the Australian continent. It has been suggested in later times that they may have had a trace of Polynesian blood. Although numerous at the time, the last of these gentle natives was to be exterminated in 1869 by the bullets, hunting dogs, and strychnine baits of the English settlers. It was one of the greatest crimes of the era of British imperialism.

On 12 February both ships entered Queen Charlotte Sound, an experience which, to Cook at least, must have been almost like coming home again. The seeds he had planted were thriving, the pigs he had turned loose had long since disappeared into the forests, and the local Maori, uneasy as to what vengeance Cook might take on them for the murder of Captain Furneaux's men, were extremely anxious to be friendly.

"Thursday 13th February.
The advantage we received by the Natives coming to live by us was not a little, as some of them went out afish-

ing every day when the weather would permit, and we generally got by exchanges a good part of the fruits of their labour: so that with what we got from them, and with our own nets and lines we seldom wanted fish, and celery, Scurvy grass and Portable soup were boiled with the Pease and Wheat for both ships companys every [day] during our whole stay and they had spruce beer for their drink: so that if any of them had contracted any seeds of the Scurvy these articles soon removed it, but when we arrived here there was only two invalids belonging to the *Resolution* on the Sick lists in both ships. Besides the people who took up their abode by us, we were occasionally visited by others whose residence was not far off, and other who lived more remote. Their articles of commerce were curiosities, Fish and Women the two first always came to a good market, which the latter did not: the Seamen had taken a kind of dislike to these people and were either unwilling or affraid to associate with them; it had a good effect as I never knew a man quit his station to go to their habitations. A connection with Women I allow because I cannot prevent it but never encourage, tho many Men are of opinion it is one of the greatest securities amongst Indians, and it may hold good when you intend to settle amongst them, but with travelers and strangers it is generally otherwise and more men are betrayed than saved by having connection with their women, and how can it be otherwise since all their Views are selfish without the least mixture of regard or attachment whatever; at least my observations which have been pretty general, have not pointed out to me one instance to the contrary.

"Amongst those occasional Visiters was a Chief named *Kahoura* who headed the party that cut off Captain Furneaux's boat and who himself killed the officer that commanded. To judge of the character of this man by what some of his Country said of him, he seemed to be a man more feared than beloved by them: many of them said he was a very bad man and importuned me to kill him and I believe they were not a little surprised that I did not, for accord[ing] to their ideas of equity this ought to have been done. But if I had followed the advice of all our pretended friends, I might have extirpated the whole race, for the people of each Hamlet or village by turns applied to me to distroy the other, a very striking proof of the divided state in which they live. We could not misunderstand them as Omai, who understood their language perfectly well, was our interpreter."

Cook's reference to the mutual enmity and jealousy existing between various factions underlines the fact that the Maori of New Zealand had inherited from the Polynesians an almost psychopathic inability to unite as one people or even cooperate peacefully among themselves on a generous scale.

The ships left New Zealand in February 1777 and sailed toward the northeast. After covering a distance of some sixteen hundred miles in that direction, they sighted several hitherto unknown islands in the tiny group that came to bear Cook's name.

Among these was the handsome island of Mangaia, lying like a green, inverted soup plate on the horizon of the sea. A boat from the *Resolution* failed to find a channel leading through the surrounding reef, and after some friendly exchanges with two dour Mangaians, Mourua and Makatu, who managed to reach the ship in a canoe, Cook left the island. A hundred miles to the north he reached and landed at Atiu, which was inhabited by a fierce and warlike people. It says much for the agreeable manners and good discipline preserved by both sides that the Atiueans received them in an unusually amiable manner.

Contrary winds now began to delay the ships so considerably that Cook came to the conclusion it would be impossible for him to reach the Bering Strait in time to carry out any appreciable exploration during the summer. He turned westward and sailed back to the hospitable Tonga or Friendly Islands, which he reached at the end of April. Here he found ample grass and water for the much-travelled and long-suffering livestock carried aboard the *Resolution*.

In August he was back in Tahiti, and the animals were finally landed, much to the relief of the crew and, no doubt, that of the animals themselves. Apart from a brief run ashore at Capetown, they had been on the ship for over a year. Omai was taken back to his native island of Huahine, where the ships' carpenters built him a house, presented him with some sheep and cattle, left him surrounded by all his other presents from England, and prepared to depart. Omai himself was most reluctant to say goodbye to his friends, to whom undoubtedly he had become most attached. A sailor named Rickman, who later wrote an account of the voyage, said of this parting:

"Omai hung round the captain's neck in all the seeming agony of a child trying to melt the heart of a reluctant parent. He twined his arms round him till Capt. Cook, unable any longer to contain himself, broke from him and retired to his cabin to indulge that natural sympathy which he could not resist, leaving Omai to dry up his tears and compose himself on the quarter deck."

The rest of the unhappy Omai's story may be told in a few words.

He died in Huahine two years later, having—according to some accounts—spent the intervening time "in inglorious indolence or wanton crime." Omai provided the first example of how the "virtues" of civilization can destroy a simple-minded Polynesian within a very short time. There was fundamentally nothing wrong with the nature of the young man. He was dazzled by the bright exterior of society life in England and lacked the perception to see the misery and want and suffering that lay beneath it—hardships unknown in tropical Huahine.

"Sunday 2nd November.

Whatever faults this Indian had they were more than over ballanced by his great good Nature and docile disposition. During the whole time he was with me I very seldom had reason to find fault with his conduct. His grateful heart always retained the highest sense of the favours he received in England nor will he ever forget those who honoured him with their protection and friendship during his stay there. He had a tolerable share of understanding, but wanted application and perseverance to exert it, so that his knowledge of things was very general and in many instances imperfect. He was not a man of much observation, there were many little arts as well as amusements amongst the people of the Friendly Islands which he might have conveyed to his own, where they probably would have been adopted, as being so much in their own way, but I never found that he used the least endeavours to make himself master of any one. This kind of indifferency is the true Character of his Nation, Europeans have visited them at times for these ten years past, yet we find neither new arts nor improvements in the old, nor have they copied after us in any one thing. We are therefore not to expect that Omai will be able to introduce many of our arts and customs amongst them or much improve those they have got. I think however he will endeavour to bring to perfection the fruits &ca we planted which will be no small acquisition. But the greatest benefit these islands will receive from Omai's travels will be in the Animals that have been left upon them, which probably they never would

have got had he not come to England; when these multiply of which I think, there is little doubt, they will equal, if not exceed any place in the known World for provisions."

The end of the year 1777 was now in sight and the time was rapidly approaching when Cook must sail on into more northern seas. He left Bora Bora in the Society Islands in December, a year and a half after the departure of the ships from England.

As the lovely islands of the Society Group faded out of sight astern, Cook must have known that he was leaving for good; that he had said a final goodbye to the careless, laughing Tahitian people in whose company he had spent the happiest days of his life. He was forty-nine years old and growing weary of the unceasing arduousness and responsibilities of his existence. Did he perhaps yearn for some escape that would enable him to spend his remaining years in the tranquil and picturesque setting of the South Pacific instead of continuing to press onward in a career that must inevitably end—as far as anyone could foretell the future—in the grey and thankless purlieus of Greenwich Hospital?

Shortly after daybreak on 24 December, when the vessels were almost on the Equator, they sighted uninhabited Christmas Island. There they captured a number of turtles, a delicacy much appreciated by sailors accustomed to the monotonous shipboard fare.

Cook had little comment to make on this discovery beyond saying that the soil was "light and black, evidently composed of decayed vegetables, the dung of birds and sand." He came to the conclusion that although it has an extent of three hundred thousand acres and is the largest of all atolls, the island had never been inhabited. Nevertheless, it was covered with coconut palms, which botanists now hold are not endemic to atoll islands; those on Christmas Island must have been transported and planted by early Polynesian voyagers. Nor would the lack of water, on which Cook commented, have precluded human habitation. The atoll islander could have cleaned his fish in sea water, replaced his soiled garments with new ones, and washed his body daily in the sea. At times a scooped-out excavation on the beach, filled by fresh-water seepage, and a coconut shell dipper provided for bodily ablution. An endless supply of green coconuts (*nū*), each holding a pint or more of cool and pleasant liquid, adequately satisfied his thirst. Shallow wells provided brackish water, palatable enough to those accustomed to it.

One thing is certain: Christmas Island will never be inhabited again. A later generation of the white race used the atoll as a base for nuclear tests.

On the morning of 18 January 1778 Cook made what was fated to be his last great discovery: he sighted Niihau and Kauai, the two most westerly islands of the Hawaiian Group.

"Monday 19th January.

At this time we were in some doubt whether or not the land before us was inhabited, this doubt was soon cleared up, by seeing some Canoes coming off from the shore towards the Ships, I immediately brought to to give them time to come up. There were three and four men in each and we were agreeably surprised to find them of the same Nation as the people of Tahiti and the other islands we had lately visited. It required but very little address to get them to come alongside, but we could not prevail upon any one to come on board. They exchanged a few fish they had in the Canoes for any thing we offered them, but valued nails, or iron above every other thing; the only weapons they had were a few stones* in some of the Canoes and these they threw overboard when they found they were not wanted. Seeing no signs of an anchoring place at this part of the island, I bore up for the lee side, and ranged the SE side at the distance of half a league from the shore. As soon as we made sail the Canoes left us, but others came off from the shore and brought with them roasting pigs and some very fine Potatoes, which they exchanged, as the others had done, for whatever was offered them; several small pigs were got for a sixpenny nail or two a piece, so that we again found ourselves in the land of plenty, just as the turtle we had taken on board at the last island was nearly expended. We passed several villages, some seated upon the sea shore and other up in the Country. The inhabitants of all of them crowded to the shore and on the elevated places to view the Ships. The land on this

Drawing of a New Zealand flax plant done on one of Cook's voyages.

side of the island rises in a gentle slope from the sea shore to the foot of the Mountains that are in the middle of the island, except in one place, near the east end where they rise directly from the sea; here they seem to be formed of nothing but stone which lay in horizontal stratas. We saw no wood but what was up in the interior part of the island and a few trees about the vil-

* Probably the basalt stone sinkers still used today for fishing out at sea.

131

CAPTIONS OF PLATES 75–90

75–79 "*At the entrance of this large morai there were high wood carved figures.*"
"*They led us to that end of the morai, where the five poles were fixed. At the foot of them were twelve images in a semicircular form.*"
"*Two little houses were situated near the Bay.*"
"*A Chief Priest superintended all religious ceremonies at the Morai. This was completely new to us. Nowhere else in the Pacific Islands we had found Societies of Priests.*"
The Marae near Honaunau on the west coast of Hawaii.

80, 81 "*The next day the Dead Body had been carried away and I could not find out what they had done with it.*"
(80) One of the many natural caves in the volcanic rock between Kiholo and Keahole Point on the west coast of Hawaii. The natives used these caves both as places of refuge in danger and sometimes as burial places.
(81) Entrance to the above-mentioned cave.

82 "*These images are made of wood and covered with small feathers.*"
An image of a Hawaiian god of war, made of a basketry framework to which feathers have been attached. The teeth are polished dog's teeth, and the eyes are mother-of-pearl. The median crest is of yellow feathers. The remainder are red, the sacred color throughout Polynesia.

83–85 and 88 "*On this side of the Island the whole ground is covered with volcanic ashes, crossed by black strips showing well where the lava of the volcano had come down. The whole southern cape seems to consist of volcanic cinders.*"
Hawaiian petroglyphs between Kiholo and Keahole Point (Plate 83, Bishop Museum, Honolulu).

86 "*This bay appears a proper place to refit the ships, and lay in an additional supply of water and provisions.*"
Kealakekua Bay on the west coast of Hawaii, where Cook was killed by the natives.

87 "*Now we got further very slowly for the ground was marshy and covered with thick copse.*"
Hawaii. Thick growths of fern thrive in the warm, moist lava-derived soil.

89 "*We judged there was a Vulcano by the Continual Column of Smoak we saw assend.*"
Hawaii. Kilauea, with the largest of all active craters. Although an independent volcano and older than Mauna Loa, Kilauea is merely a hole in the side of the latter at an elevation of 4,090 feet.

90 "*On some spots the Vegetation seemed to have been burnt down.*"
A clearance burned into the forest by hot vapors, halfway between Kokee and Kalalau in the northwest of Kauai, one of the Hawaiian Islands.

79

78

83

84

85

86 ▷

lages; we observed several Plantains and sugar canes, and places that seemed to be planted with roots.

"The next morning we stood in for the land and were met by several Canoes filled with people, some of them took courage and ventured on board. I never saw Indians so much astonished at the entering of a ship before, their eyes were continually flying from object to object, the wildness of their looks and actions fully expressed their surprise and astonishment at the several new objects before them and evinced that they never had been on board of a ship before. However, the first man that came on board did not with all surprise, forget his own interest. The first moveable thing that came in his way was the lead and line, which he without asking any questions took to put into his Canoe and when we stopped him said 'I am only going to put it into my boat,' nor would he quit until some of his countrymen spoke to him.

"At 9 o'clock being pretty near the shore, I sent three armed boats under the command of Lieutenant Williamson, to look for a landing place and fresh water. I ordered him, that if he found it necessary to land to look for the latter, not to suffer more than one man to go out of the boat. As the boats put off an Indian stole the Butcher's cleaver, leaped over board with it, got into his canoe and made for the shore. The boats pursued him but to no effect.

"As there were some venereal complaints on board both the Ships, in order to prevent its being communicated to these people, I gave orders that no Women, on any account whatever, were to be admitted on board the Ships, I also forbid all manner of connection with them, and ordered that none who had the venereal upon them should go out of the Ships. But whether these regulations had the desired effect or no, time can only discover. It is no more than what I did when I first visited the Friendly Islands, yet I afterwards found it did not succeed, and I am much afraid this will always be the case where it is necessary to have a number of people on shore. The opportunities and inducements to an intercourse between the sex, are there too many to be guarded against. It is also a doubt with me that the most skilfull of the Faculty can tell whether every man who has had the venereal is so far cured as not to communicate it further, I think I could mention some instances to the contrary. It is likewise well known that amongst a number of men, there will be found some again who care not to whom they communicate it, of this last we had an instance at Tongatabu in the Gunner of the *Discovery,* who remained ashore to manage the trade for Captain Clerke. After he knew he had contracted this disease he continued to sleep with different women who were supposed not to have contracted it; his companions expostulated with him without effect; till it came to Captain Clerke's knowledge, who ordered him on board."

The "Indians," as Cook calls them, of these islands were a virile, handsome, and extremely cultured branch of the Polynesian race, whose language and customs over the centuries had considerably diverged from those of their blood relations in the South Pacific. According to their own legends, their homeland had been discovered by an ocean voyager named Hawai'i-loa who sailed northward in his canoe from Raïatéa in the Society Group somewhere about A.D. 450. At that time the islands, like other parts of Polynesia, had been inhabited by a small, dark-skinned, and industrious people whom the Polynesians referred to as Menehune. This unknown race was gradually absorbed by the newcomers. Voyages between Raïatéa and the Hawaiian Islands were made periodically until about A.D. 1275, when they ceased altogether. When Cook discovered them, the Hawaiians had been living as an independent and separate people for some five hundred years.

Throughout Polynesia, the populations of mountainous islands invariably possessed a higher standard of culture, and perhaps of over-all intelligence as well, than the short, sturdy, and sun-darkened inhabitants of low-lying atolls. There were several ecological reasons for this difference, one being the better and more varied diet available in the "high" islands. The Hawaiians were particularly fortunate: their islands were extremely mountainous, the largely volcanic soil was most fertile, rivers were numerous, and the cooler latitude of the islands, between 20° and 22° south, tended to encourage physical and mental activity from the people.

That they were diligent and unrepentant thieves was only natural. Having no metals of their own, they were compelled to use wood, stone, and bone for all the tools and other articles necessary to maintain their subsistence economy. Iron axes, nails, knives, cloth, and even wire were as valuable in their eyes as gold to a European. Throughout the history of exploration, the races of Europe showed not the least aversion, whatever the drastic means necessary, to seizing gold for themselves. The Hawaiian natives were just behaving in the same way. 149

It was unfortunate, but perhaps inevitable, that the rapacity of the Hawaiians led almost immediately to the death of one of their number. Lieutenant Williamson and the crew of a boat from the *Resolution* were so beset by a crowd of natives that this officer gave the order to fire. One of the Hawaiians was shot dead.

After a month's stay in the leeward islands, which Cook named the Sandwich Islands after his patron, he was loath to delay any longer. He sailed on a northwesterly course on 2 February 1778 for the North American mainland.

Without doubt he was almost as reluctant to leave as were his men. Although by this time he was very familiar with the Polynesian race, the Hawaiians had created an even more favorable impression on his mind than the people of Tonga. It was perhaps natural that Cook, who was unable to swim, marvelled greatly at the natural proficiency of the people in the sea. It was quite usual, he declared, for "women with infants at the breast to come off in Canoes to look at the ships, and when the surf was so high that they could not land them in the Canoe they used to leap overboard with the child in their arms and make their way ashore through a surf that looked dreadful."

But what undoubtedly most impressed and delighted Cook, the conscientious leader of the expedition, was the fact that in these islands he had been able to secure unlimited supplies of fresh water, pigs, fowls, sweet potatoes, *taro* (a subsistence root crop), and an impressive variety of fruits. Little wonder that as they sailed into colder seas the delights of the Sandwich Islands became even more vivid in the memories of the crew.

They sighted the North American continent on 7 March 1778. The mountainous, heavily forested country was veiled in a blue mist. The ships continued northward, passing to the west of Vancouver Island without realizing that it was an island, and finally anchored in a deep inlet on its coast.

"Sunday, 29th March

At length, at nine o'clock in the morning of the 29th, as we were standing to the North East, we again saw the land, which, at noon, extended from North West by West, to East South East, the nearest part about six leagues distant. Our latitude was now 49° 29′ North, and our longitude 232° 29′ East. The appearance of the country differed much from that of the parts which we had before seen; being full of high mountains, whose summits were covered with snow. But the valleys between them, and the grounds on the sea coast, high as well as low, were covered to a considerable breadth with high, straight trees, that formed a beautiful prospect, as of one vast forest. The South East extreme of the land formed a low point, off which are many breakers, occasioned by sunken rocks. On this account it was called *Point Breakers* . . .

"We no sooner drew near the inlet than we found the coast to be inhabited; and at the place where we were first becalmed, three canoes came off to the ship. In one of these were two men, in another six, and in the third ten. Having come pretty near us, a person in one of the two last stood up, and made a long harangue, inviting us to land, as we guessed, by his gestures. At the same time, he kept strewing handfuls of feathers toward us; and some of his companions threw handfuls of a red dust or powder in the same manner. The person who played the orator, wore the skin of some animal, and held, in each hand, something which rattled as he kept shaking it. After tiring himself with his repeated exhortations, of which we did not understand a word, he was quiet; and then others took it, by turns, to say something, though they acted their part neither so long, nor with so much vehemence as the other. We observed that two or three had their hair quite strewed over with small white feathers; and others had large ones stuck into different parts of the head. After the tumultuous noise had ceased, they lay at a little distance from the ship, and conversed with each other in a very easy manner; nor did they seem to shew the least surprize or distrust. Some of them, now and then, got up, and said something after the manner of their first harangues; and one sung a very agreeable air, with a degree of softness and melody which we could not have expected; the word *haela*, being often repeated as the burden of the song. The breeze which soon after sprung up, bringing us nearer to the shore, the canoes began to come off in greater numbers; and we had, at one time, thirty-two of them near the ship, carrying from three to seven or eight persons each, both men and women. Several of these stood up in their canoes haranguing, and making gestures after the manner of our first visiters. One canoe was remarkable for a singular head, which had a bird's eye and bill, of an enormous size, painted on it; and a person who was in it, who seemed to be a Chief, was no less remarkable for his uncommon appearance; having many feathers hanging from his head, and being painted in an extraordinary manner. He held in his hand a carved bird of wood, as large as a pigeon,

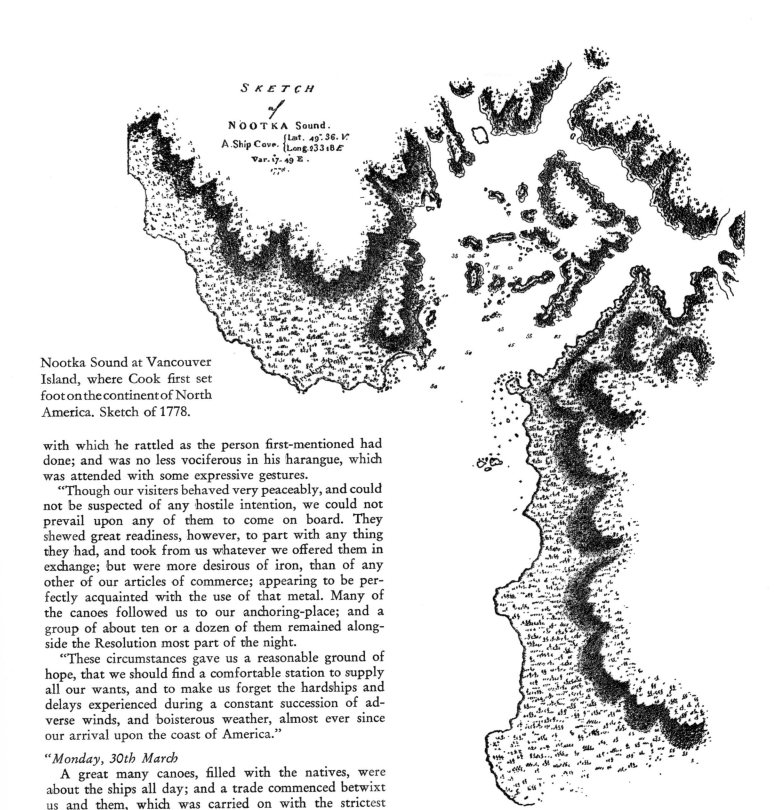

Nootka Sound at Vancouver Island, where Cook first set foot on the continent of North America. Sketch of 1778.

with which he rattled as the person first-mentioned had done; and was no less vociferous in his harangue, which was attended with some expressive gestures.

"Though our visiters behaved very peaceably, and could not be suspected of any hostile intention, we could not prevail upon any of them to come on board. They shewed great readiness, however, to part with any thing they had, and took from us whatever we offered them in exchange; but were more desirous of iron, than of any other of our articles of commerce; appearing to be perfectly acquainted with the use of that metal. Many of the canoes followed us to our anchoring-place; and a group of about ten or a dozen of them remained alongside the Resolution most part of the night.

"These circumstances gave us a reasonable ground of hope, that we should find a comfortable station to supply all our wants, and to make us forget the hardships and delays experienced during a constant succession of adverse winds, and boisterous weather, almost ever since our arrival upon the coast of America."

"*Monday, 30th March*

A great many canoes, filled with the natives, were about the ships all day; and a trade commenced betwixt us and them, which was carried on with the strictest honesty on both sides. The articles which they offered to sale were skins of various animals, such as bears, wolves, foxes, deer, rackoons, polecats, martins; and, in particular, of the sea otters, which are found at the islands East of Kamtschatka. Besides the skins in their native shape, they also brought garments made of them, and another sort of clothing made of the bark of a tree, or some plant like hemp; weapons, such as bows, arrows, and spears; fish-hooks, and instruments of various kinds;

wooden vizors of many different monstrous figures; a sort of woollen stuff, or blanketing; bags filled with red ochre; pieces of carved work; beads; and several other little ornaments of thin brass and iron, shaped like a horse-shoe, which they hang at their noses; and several chissels, or pieces of iron, fixed to handles. From their possessing which metals, we could infer that they had either been visited before by some civilized nation, or had connections with tribes on their continent, who had communication with them. But the most extraordinary of all the articles which they brought to the ships for sale, were human skulls, and hands not yet quite stripped of the flesh, which they made our people plainly understand they had eaten; and, indeed, some of them had evident marks that they had been upon the fire. We had but too much reason to suspect, from this circumstance, that the horrid practice of feeding on their enemies is as prevalent here, as we had found it to be at New Zealand and other South Sea islands. For the various articles which they brought, they took in exchange knives, chissels, pieces of iron and tin, nails, looking-glasses, buttons, or any kind of metal. Glass beads they were not fond of; and cloth of every sort they rejected."

"Tuesday, 31st March

The fame of our arrival brought a great concourse of the natives to our ships in the course of this day . . . they came on board the ships, and mixed with our people with the greatest freedom. We soon discovered, by this nearer intercourse, that they were as light-fingered as any of our friends in the islands we had visited in the course of the voyage. And they were far more dangerous thieves; for, possessing sharp iron instruments, they could cut a hook from a tackle, or any other piece of iron from a rope, the instant that our backs were turned. A large hook, weighing between twenty and thirty pounds, several smaller ones, and other articles of iron, were lost in this manner. And, as to our boats, they stripped them of every bit of iron that was worth carrying away, though we had always men left in them as a guard. They were dextrous enough in effecting their purposes; for one fellow would contrive to amuse the boat-keeper, at one end of a boat, while another was pulling out the iron work at the other. If we missed a thing immediately after it had been stolen, we found little difficulty in detecting the thief, as they were ready enough to impeach one another. But the guilty person generally relinquished his prize with reluctance; and sometimes we found it necessary to have recourse to force."

"Saturday, 18th April

On the 18th, a party of strangers, in six or eight canoes, came into the cove, where they remained, looking at us, for some time; and then retired, without coming alongside either ship. We supposed, that our old friends, who were more numerous, at this time, about us, than these new visiters, would not permit them to have any intercourse with us. It was evident, upon this and several other occasions, that the inhabitants of the adjoining parts of the Sound engrossed us entirely to themselves; or if, at any time, they did not hinder strangers from trading with us, they contrived to manage the trade for them in such a manner, that the price of their commodities was always kept up, while the value of ours was lessening every day. We also found, that many of the principal natives, who lived near us, carried on a trade with more distant tribes, in the articles they had procured from us. For we observed, that they would frequently disappear for four or five days at a time, and then return with fresh cargoes of skins and curiosities, which our people were so passionately fond of, that they always came to a good market. But we received most benefit from such of the natives as visited us daily. These, after disposing of all their little trifles, turned their attention to fishing; and we never failed to partake of what they caught. We also got from these people a considerable quantity of very good animal oil, which they had reserved in bladders. In this traffic some would attempt to cheat us, by mixing water with the oil; and, once or twice, they had the adress to carry their imposition so far, as to fill their bladders with mere water, without a single drop of oil. It was always better to bear with these tricks, than to make them the foundation of a quarrel; for our articles of traffic consisted, for the most part, of mere trifles; and yet we were put to our shifts to find a constant supply even of these. Beads, and such other toys, of which I had still some left, were in little estimation. Nothing would go down with our visiters but metal; and brass had, by this time, supplanted iron; being so eagerly sought after, that before we left this place, hardly a bit of it was left in the ships, except what belonged to our necessary instruments. Whole suits of clothes were stripped of every button; bureaus of their furniture; and copper kettles, tin cannisters, candlesticks, and the like, all went to wreck; so that our American friends here got a greater medley and variety of things from us, than any other nation whom we had visited in the course of the voyage."

"Sunday, 19th April
Monday, 20th April

After a fortnight's bad weather, the 19th proving a fair day, we availed ourselves of it, to get up the topmasts and yards, and to fix up the rigging. And, having now finished most of our heavy work, I set out the next morning to take a view of the Sound. I first went to the West point, where I found a large village, and, before it, a very snug harbour, in which was from nine to four fathoms water, over a bottom of fine sand. The people of this village, who were numerous, and to most of whom I was well known, received me very courteously; every one pressing me to go into his house, or rather his apartment; for several families live under the same roof.

I did not decline the invitations; and my hospitable friends, whom I visited, spread a mat for me to sit down upon, and shewed me every other mark of civility. In most of the houses were woman at work, making dresses of the plant or bark before mentioned, which they executed exactly in the same manner that the New Zealanders manufacture their cloth. Others were occupied in opening sardines. I had seen a large quantity of them brought on shore from canoes, and divided by measure amongst several people, who carried them up to their houses, where the operation of curing them by smoke-drying is performed. They hang them on small rods; at first, about a foot from the fire; afterward they remove them higher and higher, to make room for others, till the rods, on which the fish hang, reach the top of the house. When they are completely dried, they are taken down and packed close in bales, which they cover with mats. Thus they are kept till wanted; and they are not a disagreeable article of food. Cod, and other large fish, are also cured in the same manner by them; though they sometimes dry these in the open air, without fire.

"The persons of the natives are, in general, under the common stature; but not slender in proportion, being commonly pretty full or plump, though not muscular. Neither doth the soft fleshiness seem ever to swell into corpulence; and many of the older people are rather spare, or lean. The visage of most of them is round and full; and sometimes, also, broad, with high prominent cheeks; and, above these, the face is frequently much depressed, or seems fallen in quite across between the temples; the nose also flattening at its base, with pretty wide nostrils, and a rounded point. The forehead rather low; the eyes small, black, and rather languishing than sparkling; the mouth round, with large round thickish lips; the teeth tolerably equal and well set, but not remarkably white. They have either no beards at all, which was commonly the case, or a small thin one upon the point of the chin; which does not arise from any natural defect of hair on that part, but from plucking it out more or less; but the hair of the head is in great abundance, very coarse and strong; and, without a single exception, black, straight, and lank, or hanging down over the shoulders. The neck is short; the arms and body have no particular mark of beauty or elegance in their formation, but are rather clumsy; and the limbs, in all, are very small in proportion to the other parts, and crooked, or ill made, with large feet badly shaped, and projecting ankles. This last defect seems, in a great measure, to arise from their sitting so much on their hams or knees, both in their canoes and houses.

"Their colour we could never positively determine, as their bodies were incrusted with paint and dirt; though, in particular cases, when these were well rubbed off, the whiteness of the skin appeared almost to equal that of Europeans.

"The women are nearly of the same size, colour, and form, with the men; . . . and hardly any one was seen, even amongst those who were in the prime of life, who had the least pretensions to be called handsome.

"The natives rub their bodies constantly over with a red paint, a clayey or coarse ochry substance, mixed with oil, their garments, by this means, contract a rancid offensive smell, and a greasy nastiness. So that they make a very wretched dirty appearance; and what is still worse, their heads and their garments swarm with vermin, which, so depraved is their taste for cleanliness, we used to see them pick off with great composure, and eat.

"Though their bodies are always covered wih red paint, their faces are often stained with a black, a brighter red, or a white colour, by way of ornament. The last of these gives them a ghastly, disgusting aspect.

"They have some dress and ornaments that seem to be used only on extraordinary occasions; either when they exhibit themselves as strangers, in visits of ceremony, or when they go to war. Amongst the first may be considered the skins of animals, such as wolves or bears, tied on in the usual manner, but ornamented at the edges with broad borders of fur, or of the woollen stuff manufactured by them, ingeniously wrought with various figures. These are worn either separately, or over their other common garments. On such occasions, the most common head-dress is a quantity of withe, or half beaten bark, wrapped about the head; which, at the same time, has various large feathers, particularly those of eagles, stuck in it, or is entirely covered, or, we may say, powdered with small white feathers. The face, at the same time, is variously painted, having its upper and lower parts of different colours, the strokes appearing like fresh gashes; or it is besmeared with a kind of tallow, mixed with paint, which is afterward formed into a great variety of regular figures, and appears like carved work. Sometimes, again, the hair is separated into small parcels, which are tied at intervals of about two inches, to the end, with thread; and others tie it together, behind, after our manner, and stick branches of the *cupressus thyoides* in it. Thus dressed, they have a truly savage and incongruous appearance; but this is much heightened when they assume, what may be called, their monstrous decorations. These consist of an endless variety of carved wooden masks or vizors, applied on the face, or to the upper part of the head or forehead. Some of these resemble human faces, furnished with hair, beards, and eye-brows; others, the heads of birds, particularly of eagles and quebrantahuessos; and many, the heads of land and sea-animals, such as wolves, deer, and porpoises, and others. But, in general, these representations much exceed the natural size; and they are painted, and often strewed with pieces of the foliaceous *mica*, which makes them glitter, and serves to augment their enormous deformity. They even exceed this sometimes, and fix on the same part of the head large pieces of carved work, resembling the prow of a canoe, painted in the same manner, and projecting to a considerable distance. So fond are they of these disguises, that I have seen one of them put his head into a tin kettle he had got from us, for want of another sort of mask. Whether they use these extravagant masquerade ornaments on any particular religious occasion, or diversion; or whether they be put on to intimidate their enemies when they go to battle, by their monstrous appearance; or as decoys when they go to hunt animals, is uncertain. But it may be concluded, that, if travellers or voyagers, in an ignorant and credulous age, when many unnatural or marvellous things were supposed to exist, had seen a number of people decorated in this manner, without being able to approach so near as to be undeceived, they would readily have believed, and, in their relations, would have attempted to make others believe, that there existed a race of beings, partaking of the nature of man and beast; more especially, when, besides the heads of animals on the human shoulders, they might have seen the whole bodies of their men-monsters covered with quadrupeds' skins. This reflection may furnish the admirers of Herodotus, in particular, with an excellent apology for some of his wonderful tales of this sort."

"Wednesday, 22nd April

Captain Clerke and I went, in the forenoon, with two boats, to the village at the West point of the Sound. When I was there the day before, I had observed, that plenty of grass grew near it; and it was necessary to lay in a quantity of this, as food for the few goats and sheep which were still left on board. The inhabitants received us with the same demonstrations of friendship which I had experienced before; and the moment we landed, I ordered some of my people to begin their operation of cutting. I had not the least imagination, that the natives could make any objection to our furnishing ourselves with what seemed to be of no use to them, but was necessary for us. However, I was mistaken; for, the moment that our men began to cut, some of the inhabitants interposed, and would not permit them to proceed, saying they must *"makook"*; that is, must first buy it. I was now in one of the houses; but as soon as I heard of this, I went to the field, where I found about a dozen of the natives, each of whom laid claim to some part of the grass that grew in this place. I bargained with them for it, and having completed the purchase, thought that we were now at liberty to cut wherever we pleased. But here, again, it appeared, that I was under a mistake; for the liberal manner in which I had paid the first pretended proprietors, brought fresh demands upon me from others; so that there did not seem to be a single blade of grass, that had not a separate owner; and so many of them were to be satisfied, that I very soon emptied my pockets. When they found, that I really had nothing more to give, their importunities ceased, and we were permitted to cut wherever we pleased, and as much as we chose to carry away.

"Here I must observe, that I have no where, in my several voyages, met with any uncivilized nation, or tribe, who had such strict notions of their having a right to the exclusive property of every thing that their country produces, as the inhabitants of this Sound. At first, they wanted our people to pay for the wood and water that they carried on board; and had I been upon the spot, when these demands were made, I should certainly have complied with them. Our workmen, in my absence, thought differently; for they took but little notice of such claims; and the natives, when they found that we were determined to pay nothing, at last ceased to apply. But they made a merit of necessity; and frequently afterward, took occasion to remind us, that they had given us wood and water out of friendship."

"Thursday, 23rd April
Friday, 24th April
Saturday, 25th April

The three following days were employed in getting ready to put to sea; the sails were bent; the observatories and instruments, brewing vessels, and other things, were moved from the shore; some small spars, for different uses, and pieces of timber, which might be occasionally sawn into boards, were prepared and put on board; and both ships were cleared, and put into a sailing condition.

"Every thing being now ready . . . "

"Sunday, 26th April

Our friends, the natives, attended us, till we were almost out of the Sound; some on board the ships, and others in their canoes. One of their Chiefs, who had, some time before, attached himself to me, was amongst the last who left us. Having, before he went, bestowed upon him a small present, I received in return, a beaver-skin, of much greater value. This called upon me to make some addition to my present, which pleased him so much, that he insisted upon my acceptance of the beaver-skin cloak which he then wore; and of which I knew he was particularly fond. Struck with this instance of generosity, and desirous that he should be no sufferer by his friendship to me, I presented to him a new board-sword, with a brass hilt: the possession of which made him completely happy. He, and also many others of his countrymen, importuned us much to pay them another visit; and, by way of encouragement, promised to lay in a good stock of skins.

"On my arrival in this inlet, I had honoured it with the name of King George's Sound; but I afterward found, that it is called Nootka by the natives."

Ranging northward through miserable days of squalls and sleet, Cook progressed along the coast of Alaska.

There was no necessity to examine the coast of the mainland in detail. The unfaltering line of the snow-capped Rocky Mountains made it evident that no Northwest Passage could exist in this area.

In a latitude of 60° north the coast began to swing westward, and here the work of exploration became more serious. Bering's map, of which Cook had a copy, was incomplete and delineated only certain sections of the coast. Investigation of the estuary of the Cook River proved that it was impossible for a ship to advance more than one hundred miles up it. Thereafter, with the deck seams of the *Resolution* still leaking and the state of the masts and rigging causing considerable worry, Cook sailed through the Aleutian Islands and into the Bering Sea. On 2 August the surgeon, Mr. Anderson, died of tuberculosis. This was a serious loss, for Anderson was skilled in ethnology and anthropology and had given Cook considerable assistance during the voyage in amassing information regarding native customs.

Six days later, Cook sighted and named Cape Prince of Wales which, he noted, "is the more remarkable by being the Western extremity of all America hitherto known." By this time it was becoming evident that the chances of discovering a navigable sea passage were very remote. Cold and heavy fogs frequently obscured the coast, heavy snow squalls came hissing across the icy sea, and the land, from what glimpses of it they caught, was cold, inhospitable and barren. The second part of August was spent cautiously sailing back and forth between the coasts of Asia and America in an average latitude of 70° north, trying unsuccessfully to find a way through the ice-pack. The barrier of ice began due west of the headland he named Icy Cape, in latitude 70° 29' north, and continued to run westward until lost to sight on the cold-blurred horizon of the Chukchi Sea.

"Saturday 29 August.

The season was now so very far advanced and the time when the frost is expected to set in so near at hand, that I did not think it consistent with prudence to make any further attempts to find a passage this year in any direction, so little was the prospect of succeeding. My attention was now directed towards finding out some place where we could obtain Wood and Water, and in the considering how I should spend the Winter, so as to make some improvement to Geography and Navigation and at the same time be in a condition to return to the North in further search of a passage the ensuing summer."

Hurrying south, with leaks and faulty caulking still proving a constant worry to Clerke and Cook, the vessels put in at the island of Unalaska in the Aleutians. By that time there were three feet of water in the *Resolution*'s well, and the sails and standing rigging were so rotten that they parted in every strong wind. At Unalaska, Cook met a number of friendly and cheerful Russian fur traders who were very willing to impart information.

"The following afternoon we were visited by one *Jacob Iwanawitch,* a Russian Chief who Commanded a boat or small vessel at Oomanak. This man seemed to be the very reverse of all the other Russians; he had a great share of Modesty and would drink no strong liquor, which all the other were immoderately fond of ... After we became acquainted with these Russians some of our gentlemen at different times visited their settlement where they always met with a hearty welcome. This settlement consisted of a dwelling house and two store houses; and besides the Russians, there were a number of Kamtschatkadales and Natives, as Servants or slaves to the former, some others of the Natives, that seemed independent of the Russians, lived at the same place ... There are Russians on all the principal islands between this and *Kamtschatka,* for the sole purpose of furring, and the first and great object is the Sea Beaver or Otter; I never heard them enquire after any other Animal, not that they let any other furs Slip through their fingers when they can get them. I never thought to ask how long it was since they got a footing upon *Oonalaska* and the neighbouring isles, but to judge from the great subjection the Natives are under, it must have been some time. All these Furriers are relieved from time to time by others, those we met with came here from *Okhotsk* in 1776 and are to return in 1781, so that their stay at the island will be four years at least."

CAPTIONS OF PLATES 91–102

91, 92 *"In this part of the Island we everywhere saw signs of the devastation caused by a Vulcano."*
Hawaii. The volcano Mauna Loa.
(91) One of the craters of Mauna Loa surrounded by scorched trees.
(92) Vapors of sulphur have destroyed the vegetation.

93 *"At one corner of the house of Worship stood a rude image."*
Stone sculpture from the Sandwich (later Hawaiian) Islands (Bishop Museum, Honolulu).

94 *"They have a lot of grotesque wooden images."*
Pele, the Hawaiian goddess of volcanic fires, seen here with human hair and eyes of mother-of-pearl. Pele was said to have traveled from island to island searching for a place to live. At last she burrowed into the great volcano Kilauea on the island of Hawaii, and there she stayed (British Museum).

95, 99 und 101 *"All these are looked upon as signs of the vicinity of land. However, we discovered none till daybreak, when an island made its appearance."*
"The mountains, which occupy the centre of the country seemed to be formed of nothing but stone, or rocks lying in horizontal strata."
Kauai was the island Cook discovered first of all the Sandwich Islands.

(95) Waimea Canyon in the southwest of Kauai.
(99) Fern grotto near the Wailua River in eastern Kauai.
(101) View from the coast toward the ocean.

96 *"The shore was of black vulcanic sand."*
One of the lovely bays of Hawaii.

97, 98 *"The ground was covered with bushes and plants of such sweet smell I have found in no other island of this region."*
(97) A blossom which is used by the natives as an ornament, but they also extract a dye from it.
(98) Crab flower.

100 *"We were led in a large house, were we met a black human figure resting on his toes and fingers, and his head backward, the limbs were well proportioned, and the whole was beautifully polished."*
A carved wooden figure from the mausoleum of the House of King Kaewe at Honaunau, Hawaii. The eyes are of mother-of-pearl (British Museum).

102 *"There were often clouds raising from the mountains which gave the island enough rain; reaching the sea they vanished in the sky."*
The Pacific Ocean to the east of Hawaii.

94

93

97

98

RETURN TO HAWAII

hile the officers and passengers hobnobbed with the Russians, the *Resolution* and *Discovery* were overhauled and thoroughly repaired. It was not before it was well needed.

"The Carpenters belonging to both Ships were set to work to rip off the Sheathing and under the Wale on the Starboard side abaft, where many of the Seams were found quite open, so that it was no wonder that so much water found its way into the Ship. While we lay here we cleared the Fish room, Spirit room and after hold, disposed things in such a manner that if we should happen to have any more leaks of the same Nature the Water might find its way to the pumps. And besides this work compleating our Water, we cleared the Fore hold to the very bottom and took in a quantity of ballast.

"The Vegetables we met with when first at this place were mostly in a state of decay, so that we benefited but little by them; but this loss was more than made up by the great quantity of berries everywhere found ashore, and in order that we might benefit as much as possible by them, one third of the people by turns had leave to go and pick them and besides a good quantity were procured from the Natives; so that if there was any seeds of the Scurvy in either ship, these berries and Spruce beer which they had to drink every other day, effectually removed it. We also got plenty of fish, at first from the Inhabitants, mostly Salmon both fresh and dryed; some of the fresh salmon was one sort which we called hook nosed from the figure of its head, that was but indifferent."

Even after all these repairs to the ships had been completed, unsuspected weaknesses still remained. Iron securing bolts were rust-eaten, eyebolts still inclined to pull adrift from canvas, and footropes were rotten at the core. When the ships sailed from Unalaska on 26 October, many of these hidden dangers had not been discovered. That same evening, while running westward to overcome a brisk southerly wind, tragedy occurred aboard the *Discovery*. A parral, the collar by which a yard is held to a mast, suddenly snapped and the ponderous wooden yard broke free from the mast. In its crashing descent it killed one man, severely injured the boatswain, and caused lesser injuries to three other sailors.

On 25 November Cook sighted the hitherto unknown island of Maui, lying to the east of Kauai in the Sandwich Islands. Being unable to find an anchorage, and as the "dreadful surf" prevented the dispatch of a boat to the shore, Cook altered course to the southward. On 30 November he sighted another island. By that time a number of the islanders had reached the *Resolution* aboard their handsome sailing canoes, and from these people Cook learned that the name of this new island was Hawaii. Not until several days later, however, did he become aware that it was the largest and most important of the Group.

"*Wednesday 2nd December.*

We were surprised to see the summits of the highest [mountains] cover[ed] with snow; they did not appear to be of any extraordinary height and yet in some places the snow seemed to be of considerable depth and to have laid there some time. As we drew near the shore, some of the Natives came off to us; they were a little shy at first, but we soon enticed some on board and at length prevailed upon them to go ashore and bring off what we wanted. Soon after these reached the shore we had company enough, and as few came empty, we got a tolerable supply of small pigs, fruit, and roots. We continued trading with them till Six in the evening when we made sail and stood off, with a view of plying to windward round the island."

The stocks of rum aboard the ships were becoming low after two and a half years away from England, and in order to conserve what remained Cook decided to replace the daily ration to the crew with the beer he had brewed from sugar-cane brought aboard by the Hawaiians. But when he broached a cask, none of the sailors would drink it.

The fact of the matter was that Cook, his officers, and the crews of both vessels were tired after their frustrating search for the Northwest Passage and therefore in an irascible mood. Cook's peevish entry in the Journal for 2 December indicates this fact. It was the first occasion during his three voyages that he had been harassed by trouble with his crew and it came at an unfortunate time.

"As I had no motive for doing it but to save our spirit for a Colder climate, I gave myself no trouble either to oblige or persuade them to drink it, knowing there was no danger of the Scurvy as long as we had plenty of other Vegetables; but that I might not be disappointed in my views I gave orders that no grog Should be served in either ship. Myself and the Officers continued to make use of this beer whenever we could get cane to make it; a few hops, of which we had on board, was a great addition to it: it has the taste of new malt beer, and I believe no one will doubt it must be very wholesome, though my turbulent crew alleged it was injurious to their healths. [*A strange point of view. Later generations of passing sailors gladly drank the beer. RS*] ... Every innovation whatever, tho ever so much to their advantage, is sure to meet with the highest disapprobation from Seamen, Portable Soup and Sauerkraut were at first both condemned by them as stuff not fit for human beings to eat. Few men have introduced into their Ships more novelties in the way of victuals and drink than I have done; indeed few men have had the same opportunity or been driven to the same necessity. It has however in a great measure been owing to such little innovations that I have always kept my people generally speaking free from that dreadful distemper the Scurvy."

After surveying the coast of Hawaii from 30 November 1778 until 17 January 1779, and becoming more impressed all the time with the beauty and great fertility of the island, as well as the natural honesty and guilelessness of the people—both qualities being more pronounced than with the Tahitians—the ships finally anchored in Kealakekua Bay on the western side of Hawaii.

The principal gods of the Hawaiian people were Kane (Tane), Ku (Tu), Lono (Ro'o, Rongo), and Kanaloa (Ta'aroa, Tangaroa), derived directly from Tahiti. News of the appearance of the ships some months earlier had been eagerly circulated, not only in Niihau and Kauai but also in the other six easterly islands of the group. By some of the people it was supposed that Cook himself, who had made a great impression with his tall, distinguished figure, was Lono, the god of plenty. By others, his dark brown hair, austere features, and obvious position of command were taken to indicate at least his kinship with Kanaloa the supreme god.* The people attached

* So completely did later missionaries destroy Hawaiian mythology that the surviving remnant of the race interpret Kane, Ku and Lono as the Trinity, while Kanaloa is wrongly and unhappily regarded as the Devil.

great significance to the fact that the ships anchored in Kealakekua Bay which, according to legend, was the special abode of Kanaloa. For this reason, the towering cliffs fringing the shore contained the tombs of many of the chiefs. On the surrounding hills were a number of *marae*, sacred stone-bordered enclosures of impressive size and dignity that were used as temples. Obviously, declared the people, Lono (or Kanaloa) had come home to his people.

The arrival of the ships was thus regarded as a tremendous religious occasion. The Hawaiian priests themselves were convinced that Cook was a god and therefore encouraged the excited religious fervor of their people. The ships were almost swamped by vast crowds of people who came out, swimming or in canoes, to welcome them. Thus also the reason for the sudden prevalence of theft amongst the islanders who, during Cook's visit to the two leeward islands, had impressed him with their unusual honesty: now they were overcome with eagerness to seize relics, particularly anything made of iron which they regarded as a rare, beautiful, and sacred metal.

"*Sunday 17th January.*
... The ship was very much crowded with Indians and surrounded by a multitude of canoes. I have nowhere in this sea seen such a number of people assembled at one place, besides those in the Canoes all the Shore of the bay was covered with people and hundreds were swimming about the Ships like shoals of fish. We should have found it difficult to have kept them in order had not a Chief ... named Parea now and then [exerted] all his authority by turning or rather driving them all out of the Ships. Among our numerous visitors was a man named Tou-ah-ah, who we soon found belonged to the Church. He introduced himself with much ceremony, in the Course of which he presented me with a small pig, two coconuts and a piece of red cloth which he wrapped round me: in this manner all or most of the chiefs or people of Note introduce themselves, but this man went farther, he brought with him a large hog and a quantity of fruits and roots all of which he included in the present.
"In the afternoon I went ashore to view the place, accompanied by Tou-ah-ah, Parea, Mr. King and others; as soon we landed Tou-ah-ah took me by the hand and conducted me to a large *marae*, the other gentlemen with Parea and four or five more of the natives followed."

(Some forty years later, an American so-called missionary named Bingham wrote: "How vain, rebellious, and at the same time contemptible for a worm to presume to receive homage and sacrifices from the stupid and polluted worshippers of demons and of the vilest objects of creation...without one note of remonstration of the dishonour cast on the Almighty Creator." The missionary chose to ignore the fact that Cook was in entire ignorance at the time of the significance of the proceedings on the *marae*.)

The fair copy of Cook's Journal ended soon after sighting Hawaii on 30 November. He continued to maintain his rough Journal until the evening of 17 January when the ships were anchored in Kealakekua Bay. This explains the terse style and the absence of observant details in the above extract from the rough Journal. The language of an explorer is always curt of necessity, but frequently there were times when Cook was able to describe an impressive scene in well-chosen and evocative words. The sequel is therefore told in the words of Lieutenant (later Captain) King, and culminates in the report made by Lieutenant Phillips who commanded the Marines.

Within a few days of the arrival of the ships, the Hawaiians were beginning to have first doubts about the divine origin of their visitors. True, their supreme chief, the aged King Kalniopu, had been escorted out to the *Resolution* by four large and splendid canoes and had signified his approval and friendship by being paddled round the anchored vessels with impressive dignity before returning ashore. But certain other facts were beginning to distress the Hawaiian people.

The sailors were over-amorous in their attitude towards even the most high-born women, and the husbands were jealous and incensed by this lack of respect. Nor was it in keeping with the supposed divine origin of these white-skinned strangers that they should consort on the most intimate terms with females of the lowest class. Then there was the question of the enormous quantities of hogs, exquisite feather capes, carved ceremonial adzes, fruit, vegetables, and other gifts which had been showered on the visitors. Even on this large and fertile island, such supplies were not inexhaustible. The Hawaiians gave, and gave generously, but they began to worry as their own resources were depleted. This was a very special occasion indeed, and they regarded it as such, but they hoped secretly that the occasion was not going to develop into a permanent residence of the white god and his somewhat earthy companions.

The disillusioning process really began on 1 February. An old seaman named Watman died and was buried ashore. This, according to a perceptive Swiss sailor named Zimmerman, "destroyed their previous belief in our immortality, and this being lost, their reverence for us was gone."

The reaction was inevitable. The Hawaiians began recouping themselves by stealing portable articles from the ships, principally iron spikes, knives, and anything made of copper.

"They supposed," wrote King, "we had left our native country on account of the scantiness of provisions and that we had visited them for the sole purpose of filling our bellies."

The people found it hard to dissimulate their relief when Cook announced his intention of leaving. In a mood of great enthusiasm they gave a final feast to which Cook and Lieutenant King were invited. The following morning, 4 February, the ships departed.

It was Cook's intention to carry out a complete survey of the Hawaiian Group and to prepare a chart of them. He also wanted to find a safer anchorage than that of Kealakekua Bay, which gave little or no protection from westerly winds, before attempting to carry out repairs to both vessels.

Three days after leaving Hawaii, the ships ran into a gale. The *Resolution*'s foremast was badly sprung, and Cook decided that it would be necessary to return to the Bay in order to fell a suitable tree and shape it into a new mast. On 11 February, when the islanders were undoubtedly still rejoicing at the departure of the "hungry gods," they saw to their great dismay both vessels again entering the bay and preparing to anchor.

This time the beach was ominously quiet and deserted. No eager welcoming crowds stood gazing down from the reddish-grey volcanic cliffs; no slender canoes darted out to welcome the returning strangers.

"We were employed the whole of the 11th and part of the 12th," wrote Lieutenant King, "in getting out the foremast and sending it with the carpenters on shore. Besides the damage which the head of the mast had sustained, we found the heel exceedingly rotten .... It was not, however, thought necessary to shorten it; and fortunately the logs of red *toa*-wood [ironwood. RS] which had been cut at Eimeo [Moorea in the Society Islands] for anchor-stocks, were found fit to replace the sprung part of the fishes. As these repairs were likely to take up several days, Mr. Bayly [the astronomer] and myself got the astronomical apparatus on shore, and pitched our tents on the *marae*; having with us a guard of a corporal and six marines .... Upon our coming to anchor we were surprised to find our reception very different from what it had been on our first arrival; no shouts, no bustle, no confusion, but a solitary bay, with only here and there a canoe stealing close along the shore."

The setting up of tents and all the other indications of a lengthy stay by the visitors depressed the Hawaiians still further. Similarly the sailors, who had naturally come to regard themselves as persons of importance on this delectable island, were disappointed by the manner in which the local population had begun to shun them. In other words, there were incipient bad feelings and resentment on both sides.

On 13 February the tense atmosphere between the two races resulted in an unfortunate incident. Several Hawaiians were helping a watering party of sailors to roll the filled wooden casks to the boats. Several minor chiefs appeared and ordered their men to stop work and move away. Apparently at the same time, some other Hawaiians began to pick up lumps of lava rock and adopted a threatening attitude. Lieutenant King, who was in command of the watering party, reported this fact to Cook, who was just stepping ashore from another boat. On the direct order of Cook himself, the six Marine sentries removed the bird-shot from their muskets and reloaded with solid .750 lead ball.

Peace seems to have been temporarily restored at this stage, but almost immediately another and more serious incident occurred. A prowling Hawaiian aboard the *Discovery* snatched up a couple of iron tools belonging to the armorer, ran to the side of the ship, and jumped into a waiting canoe.

Several musket shots were fired from the deck of the *Discovery* at the fleeing canoe but without doing any damage. Cook and King, who were still on shore, heard the shots and hastened to the beach to intercept the approaching canoe, which by this time was being pursued by a boat from the *Discovery*. Mr. Edgar, master of the *Discovery*, and Midshipman Vancouver, both of whom had accompanied the boat, found the canoe being drawn up on the beach. They seized the thief, who promptly broke free and escaped inland, but they successfully recovered the stolen tools.

Edgar then decided to seize the canoe and tow it back to the ship. Parea, to whom the canoe belonged, arrived at that moment and protested by signs that he knew nothing of the theft. He snatched up a paddle to defend his property and was knocked down by a sailor with an oar. A general scuffle between seamen and Hawaiians then took place, in which the *Discovery*'s men had very much the worst of it. Parea eventually managed to stop the fight and apologized for what had happened.

When Cook learned of this fracas, he realized immediately that he and his crew had again "lost face" by the incidents. No one would regard them any longer as being even remote relations of the gods.

"I am afraid," he said to King, "that these people will oblige me to use some violent measures, for they must not be left to imagine that they have gained an advantage over us."

At daybreak the following morning, 14 February 1779, Lieutenant Burney reported that the *Discovery*'s cutter had been removed during the night. The painter attaching it to the ship's side had been cut.

When this theft was reported to Cook, the Marines were ordered to parade and load their muskets with ball. Cook himself picked up his

173

double-barrelled shotgun and loaded one barrel with bird-shot, the other with solid shot. He told King that he proposed to seize a hostage on shore and bring him aboard the *Resolution* until the cutter was restored. He appeared to his subordinate as being in a hasty, determined, and extremely angry mood.

Two boats accompanied Cook to the shore, the *Resolution*'s pinnace commanded by Mr. Roberts, the master, and a launch under Lieutenant Williamson. The nine Marines composing the guard were under the command of Lieutenant Phillips. Cook also ordered Lieutenant King to take a boat to a spot further along the bay.

"The last orders I received from him," wrote King, "were to quiet the minds of the natives on our side of the bay by assuring them they should not be hurt; to keep my people together and to be on my guard."

Cook landed on the beach, accompanied by nine Marines and their officer, leaving the boats a few yards out from the shore in shallow water. He walked some fifty yards inland to the thatched house of the old king, Kalaniopu, who was still asleep on the thick and comfortable mat used by Polynesian people. The time was then approximately 8:00 A.M.

What transpired inside that hut will never be made clear. One must accept with a grain of salt the Journal's statement that "the king readily assented and immediately got up to accompany him." The fact remains that presently Cook reappeared in the low doorway, holding the old man by the hand—a sacrilege which undoubtedly shocked the crowd of several hundred Hawaiians who had now assembled on the rocky ground between the house and the beach. At the same time, several blank shots were fired as a warning by the 12-pounder guns aboard the *Resolution*.

"An elderly woman..., one of the king's favourite wives, came after him and with many tears and entreaties, besought him not to go on board. At the same time two Chiefs, who came along with her, laid hold of him, and insisting that he should go no farther, forced him to sit down. The natives, who were collecting in prodigious

numbers along the shore, and had probably been alarmed by the firing of the great guns, and the appearances of hostility in the bay, began to throng round Captain Cook and their king. In this situation, the Lieutenant of marines, observing that his men were huddled close together in the crowd, and thus incapable of using their arms, if any occasion should require it, proposed to the Captain, to draw them up along the rocks, close to the Water's edge; and the crowd readily making way for them to pass, they were drawn up in a line, at the distance of about thirty yards from the place where the king was sitting.

"All this time the old king remained on the ground, with the strongest marks of terror and dejection in his countenance; Captain Cook, not willing to abandon the object for which he had come on shore, continuing to urge him in the most pressing manner, to proceed; whilst on the other hand, whenever the king appeared inclined to follow him, the Chiefs who stood round him interposed, at first with prayers and entreaties, but afterward having reccourse to force and violence, and insisted on his staying where he was. Captain Cook therefore finding that the alarm had spread too generally, and that it was in vain to think any longer of getting him off without bloodshed, at last gave up the point; observing to Mr. Phillips that it would be impossible to compel him to go on board, without the risk of killing a great number of the inhabitants."

It would be impossible for even the most determined apologist to exonerate Cook from blame in this culminating tragedy. One can merely submit mitigating circumstances for his action. For one thing, he was undoubtedly tired, harassed, and irritable, as shown by the harsh strictures he passed on his crew in the Journal entry of 2 December. For another, the theft of the cutter was a most serious loss and its recovery a matter of considerable importance. Cook was a strict disciplinarian, and beneath his unfailing attitude of tolerance and consideration for others, particularly insofar as the races of the Pacific were concerned, he had a harsh and unbending temper as his crew was well aware. The deliberate theft of the boat had aroused his wrath. He reacted as most men of that high-handed imperial age would have done by adopting extremely drastic measures which inevitably infuriated the Hawaiian people.

Cook might have succeeded in safely withdrawing by himself at this stage to the water's edge, where the Marines were already levelling their long muskets, had it not been for an unfortunate combination of events: at that moment news reached the crowd that the boat commanded by Lieutenant King had reached the shore some distance away. The men aboard it had already opened fire and killed a senior *al'ii* (chieftain). This news enraged the mass of people gathered round the king's house.

An excited man threatened Cook with an iron-tipped spear (the iron being a gift from the *Resolution*). Cook—and who can blame him?—immediately raised his gun and fired the barrel containing bird-shot at the warrior. The charge did not penetrate the latter's shield and, being greatly emboldened, he came on again. Cook then fired the second barrel loaded with ball but killed another man in error. Phillips was stabbed between the shoulders at the same moment but unhesitatingly shot his attacker dead.

Showers of stones began to fly, and at the same moment the Marines fired a volley into the crowd. The men in the boats, although armed, were unable to shoot at Cook's nearest assailants since the Marines, being forced to stand erect while engaged in the act of reloading, screened the line of fire. The boats therefore fired somewhat wildly and indiscriminately.

"Our unfortunate Commander, the last time he was seen distinctly, was standing at the water's edge, and calling out to the boats to cease firing, and to pull in. If it be true, as some of those who were present have imagined, that the marines and boatmen had fired without his orders, and that he was desirous of preventing any further bloodshed, it is not improbable, that his humanity on this occasion, proved fatal to him. For it was remarked that whilst he faced the natives, none of them had offered him any violence, but that having turned about, to give his orders to the boats, he was stabbed in the back and fell with his face in the water. On seeing him fall, the islanders set up a great shout, and his body was immediately dragged on shore, and surrounded by the enemy, who snatching the dagger out of each other's hands shared a savage eagerness to have a share in his destruction."

The fight lasted ten minutes. Captain Cook and four Marines lay dead on the beach. The rest of the Marines plunged into the sea, accompanied by the wounded Phillips, and managed to reach the over-loaded pinnace commanded by Mr. Roberts. Phillips, in spite of his own serious injury, helped another wounded Marine into the boat.

The unfortunate Lieutenant Williamson is often stated to have lost his nerve. Instead of approaching the shore, the launch he commanded moved farther out. Yet it is difficult to blame him: had he rowed towards the beach, the ten or twelve men in his boat would have been immediately massacred by the great crowd of warriors who had now gathered on the shore in an uncontrollable mood of battle frenzy. Smoothbore muskets, which took a minute to reload, and Williamson's cutlass would have been insignificant weapons in the face of such odds.

The boats hastily returned to their respective ships. The guns of both vessels opened fire and soon cleared the beach of warriors.

Later that afternoon King bravely went ashore with a flag of truce but was unable to recover Cook's body or even his uniform. That night the Hawaiians burnt the corpse on a funeral pyre in the hills. During the next few days, however, a period of intermittent suspicion and further hostilities, Clerke and King managed to recover part of Cook's skull, the arms and thigh-bones, and the hands, none of which had been consumed by the flames. One hand was recognizable by the scar on it from the powder explosion years before.

Contrary to a former belief, the Hawaiians did not eat any of the corpse and expressed the most shocked indignation when questioned on this matter. As in many Polynesian islands where semi-wild pigs provided an adequate supply of fresh meat, cannibalism was decreasing, being reserved mainly for special religious rites, before the advent of the European.

"The next morning [21 February], Eappo, and the king's son, came on board and brought with them the remaining bones of Captain Cook; the barrels of his gun, his shoes, and some other trifles that belonged to him. Eappo took great pains to convince us the Terreeoboo [King Kalaniopu], Maiha-Maiha, and himself were most

175

heartily desirous of peace; that they had given us the most convincing proof of it in their power; and that they had been prevented from giving it sooner by the other Chiefs, many of whom were still our enemies. He lamented, with the greatest sorrow, the death of six Chiefs we had killed, some of whom, he said, were amongst our best friends. The cutter, he told us, was taken away by Parea's people; very probably in revenge for the blow that had been given him; and that it had been broken up the next day. The arms of the marines, which we had also demanded, he assured us, had been carried off by the common people, and were irrecoverable."

Cook's sad relics were committed to the bay with a full ceremony of Naval honors, a solemn occasion on which all the Hawaiians were requested to withdraw from the bay, a request which they honorably observed.

By this time mutual regret for the tragedy was being expressed by both sides and an uneasy though workable relationship was restored between them. The *Resolution*'s mast was recovered and successfully stepped. Captain Clerke took over the command of the expedition and removed aboard the *Resolution*. Lieutenant Gore, the first lieutenant of that ship, was appointed Captain of the *Discovery*. Clerke, although a very sick man, proposed to put into operation Cook's plans for a continued search for the Northwest Passage. He sailed on 22 February 1779, the day after the funeral.

The ships proceeded north to the Kamchatka Peninsula on the Asiatic side of the Bering Strait and put in at the Russian port of Petropavlovsk, where Russians accorded them a friendly welcome. A letter was dispatched overland to the Admiralty with the news of Cook's death. Thus it happened that the tidings were published in English newspapers a full six months before the ships arrived home.

Clerke then made a gallant effort to reach a more northerly point than Cook had done the previous year. At a latitude of 70° 33′ north, fifteen miles short of that point, ice conditions which seemed worse than in 1778 made any further progress impossible.

"I will not endeavour to conceal the joy," wrote King, "that brightened the countenance of every individual, as soon as Captain Clerke's resolutions were made known. We were all heartily sick of a navigation full of danger, and in which the utmost perseverance had not been repaid with the smallest probability of success. We therefore turned our faces toward home, after an absencec of three years, with a delight and satisfaction, which notwithstanding the tedious voyage we had still to make, and the immense distance we had to run, were as freely entertained, and perhaps as fully enjoyed, as if we had been already in sight of the Land's-end."

But one more tragedy was destined to mar still further this fateful voyage. By early August it was clear that thirty-eight-year-old Captain Clerke was dying. He passed away as his ship was entering the harbor at Petropavlovsk, and was buried ashore in a churchyard.

Captain John Gore, the Pacific veteran who had served in two of Cook's voyages, promoted King to command the *Discovery*. Both vessels reached England on 6 October 1780. The voyage had lasted four years and three months.

The *Resolution* had lost only five men by sickness, and the *Discovery* none. Gore later became a post captain and died in 1798. Lieutenant King died in 1784, largely as a result of the hardships encountered in the vain search for a Northwest Passage. Many years later, Captain (formerly Lieutenant) Williamson was court-martialled for cowardice at the Battle of Copenhagen and dismissed from the service.

THE WHITE RACES TAKE OVER

he expedition's return attracted tremendous interest, but the event was beclouded by the death of its leader and the frustrating war with the American colonies. Thus the journal compiled by Cook and finished by King did not appear in published form until 1784.

By that time Mrs. Cook was receiving an adequate pension of £ 200 a year from the Navy Board, augmented by half the royalties accruing from the Journal of the Third Voyage. Of her six children, none survived the normal span of life. Elizabeth died in childhood during the voyage of the *Endeavour*, and two infant sons died in 1768 and 1772. Of the remaining three sons, Nathaniel became a Naval officer but was drowned in a hurricane that sank his ship, H.M.S. *Thunderer*, off Jamaica in 1780. Hugh, born in 1776, died in 1793 while a student at Cambridge University. The last son, James, rose to be a commander in the Navy but was drowned at Portsmouth in 1794. It was remarkable that in the face of so many tragedies, Mrs. Cook survived as a gracious and dignified woman, respected by all who met her, until 1835, when she had attained the age of ninety-three years.

Dr. J. C. Beaglehole, the leading historian, wrote that the map of the Pacific is Cook's ample panegyric. Professor Christopher Lloyd of the Royal Naval College, Greenwich, stated that Cook's character was adequately summarized in the names of the ships he commanded: *Resolution* and *Endeavour*, *Adventure* and *Discovery*. To these well-merited tributes, it might be added that Cook demonstrated to the navies of the world how to avoid scurvy, to navigate with infinitely more accuracy than in earlier days by means of the chronometer, and to produce charts that were worthy of the highest skill of the professional hydrographer. "He is a right-minded and unaffected man," declared a Fellow of the Royal Society who met Cook, "and I have great authority for calling him our best navigator."

The Pacific Ocean was now open to all those who cared to sail upon it.

The end of the War of American Independence stimulated British interest in the acquisition of new territories overseas. Captain Arthur Phillip arrived in Botany Bay in 1788 with the first penal ships carrying eight hundred prisoners and three hundred soldiers. From this ignominious beginning gradually arose the great and flourishing country of Australia.

After the year 1800 British, American, and French whalers were fishing regularly off the coast of New Zealand. By 1814 the gospel was preached in New Zealand for the first time. Those who undertook to convert the Maori were mostly ill-educated and untrained evangelists. They squabbled amongst themselves, and frequently fell by the wayside. Despite this unpromising start, the first officially recognized British colonists reached New Zealand in 1840, by which time the brutal behavior of sealers, deserters, and runaway convicts had aroused the Maori tribes to warlike resentment.

The London Missionary Society, a Calvinist organization founded in England, landed its first missionaries in Tahiti in 1797. Some twenty years later, the Society was establishing itself in the first of the Hervey Islands (later renamed the Cook Islands).

American missionaries reached the Hawaiian Islands in 1820, after Britain had refused to take them under her official protection. In 1898, America formally annexed the islands. Similarly Britain refused to claim the Society Islands as a protectorate, and French formal annexation of the Group, as well as of the Marquesas, took place in 1880.

After a bitter political and strategic rivalry, Samoa was partitioned between the Germans and Americans in 1899. Efficient German rule of the more attractive Western Samoa lasted until 1914, when New Zealand troops occupied the islands. From 1921 to 1946, New Zealand administered the territory under a mandate from the League of Nations in a manner described by one distinguished present-day writer as being "with good intentions but deplorable tactics." (These tactics included the fatal machine-gunning of the unarmed paramount chieftain, Tamasese, and some nine of his sub-chiefs in 1930.)

The Tonga Group, so beloved by Cook, were spared the ignominy of administration by a bumbling colonial government. They held out for their continued independence and they got it. The Group became a protectorate of Britain in 1900, and Britain has been wise enough to leave well alone. Although Tonga has lost much of its traditional way of life, it continues to flourish under the aegis of a forthright and sagacious Polynesian royal family. "Even today," wrote Dr. Hendrik van Loon in *The Story of the Pacific*, "this part of the Pacific gives the traveller the feeling that he has come upon the only healthy remnant of the old Polynesian civilization."

With Tonga, Dr. van Loon might have included the remote Gilbert and Ellice Islands a thousand miles to the north. There again, under unusually enlightened administration by Britain, the Polynesians of these widely scattered islands have been encouraged to govern themselves as much as possible, diligently protected in the process from the wiles of the rapacious trader, the would-be beachcomber, and—more lately—those of the Pacific travel agencies.

Of Tahiti, the capital of the Society Group and perhaps the fairest of them all, the less said the better. It has sunk pretty low, assisted in the process by an avaricious and picaresque French bureaucracy.

The Marquesas, inhabited in Cook's day by perhaps one hundred thousand of the finest Polynesians he had come across, have been reduced to a scant three thousand. Two wars against French troops armed with breech-loading rifles destroyed their best menfolk; the rum and opium with which the survivors were paid as semi-slave labor on French plantations in the latter half of the nineteenth century brought about the final degradation.

Were Cook to revisit the islands of the Pacific today, he would still recognize many that he charted two hundred years ago. But he would not recognize their inhabitants; in this modern age they exist only in Kodacolor in the flamboyant pamphlets of

airlines and shipping companies. And even they usually reveal distinct traces of Chinese, Negro, Japanese, or white blood.

For the fact remains that the Polynesian is a member of a rapidly disappearing race. Peruvian slaveships of the nineteenth century, tuberculosis, venereal disease, liquor, canned foodstuffs, and a money economy destroyed this pleasure-loving yet picturesque people.

The islander must take at least some of the blame for his inability to cope with the modern world. Centuries of easy living in a genial climate, after his ancestors had been compelled to endure the hardships and dangers of a seafaring existence, caused him to reach a stage when all sense of personal initiative and ambition vanished.

But in the case of Polynesia, the natural process of disintegration was accelerated by the advent of that commercialized brand of Christianity which had narrow-minded and humorless Calvinist missionaries as its emissaries. A heavy share of the blame must be laid on their unbending shoulders.

Even as long ago as 1888, the dire effects of the labors of these apostles of hellfire and brimstone were ably portrayed by a responsible British official named Mr. F. J. Moss.

"The pregnant fact forces itself into prominence that in many of the islands where Christianity is most loudly professed, there is still a dangerous void. The old amusements and dances were sternly repressed in the early days as relics of heathenism; but no healthy recreation was given in their place. The minds of the people are a perfect blank. They have no literature, no books, nothing to move the intellect or to please the taste, nothing on which a healthy progress can be based.... They need a healthy public opinion to replace the rigid laws and systems of espionage which now exist."

This stringent criticism has been confirmed in more modern times by Professor J. C. Beaglehole, who wrote:

"The mission theocracy at the height of its power in Rarotonga and Aitutaki—perhaps from 1835 to 1880—was supported by what we would today call a police state: a rigid code of laws; penalties for breaking the law levied in cash and trade goods, fines that were divided equally among police, judge and chief; espionage and 'snooping' to increase the number of convictions; fanatical carrying out of physical punishments; a proportion of police to 'Civilians' that ranged from one to twelve in Mangaia to one to six in one district of Rarotonga—in sum, a series of extremely severe infringements on the private lives and freedoms of the individual that were enforced with all the zealous enthusiasm that characterizes most converts to a militant theology and a Christian soldiery."

The comment might be made in passing that to have preserved the rare and beautiful native artifacts and culture, to have maintained the vast and beautiful *marae* found in all the islands of Polynesia, would have constituted an infinitely greater tribute to the record and achievements of these over-zealous salesmen of Heaven.

European exploitation of Polynesia, a process still in operation, constitutes one of the great tragedies of history—a tragedy with few to grieve.

Yet the fact remains that by and large the Polynesian has accepted the gasoline and plastic world of the European, the good with the bad, in whole-hearted manner. Along with his hastily discarded culture, he prefers to forget his former simple existence in a thatched cottage beside the lagoon.

"*Not one of the Natives made the least opposition to our landing but came to us with all imaginable marks of friendship and submission.*"

A plant used by Tahitians to catch fish. It contains a kind of narcotic that, released in water, stuns fish long enough for them to be gathered up.

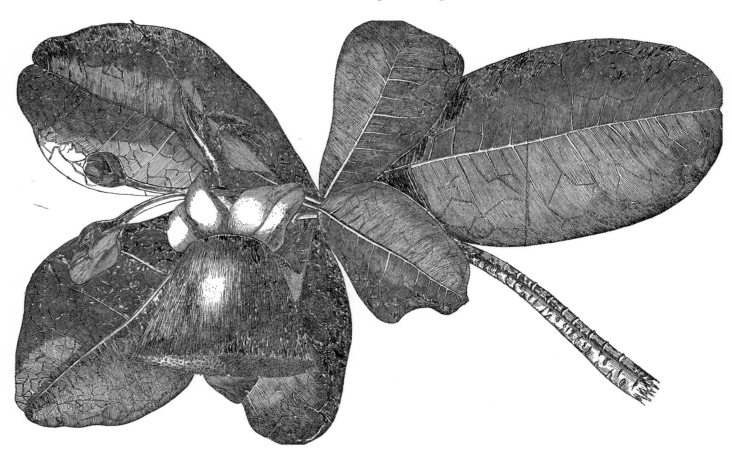